MW00887683

War and Religion

By
Mike Bhangu

BBP
Copyright 2016

www.mikebhangu.com

Copyright © 2016 by Mike Singh Bhangu.

This book is licensed and is being offered for your personal enjoyment only. It is prohibited for this book to be re-sold, shared and/or to be given away to other people. If you would like to provide and/or share this book with someone else please purchase an additional copy. If you did not personally purchase this book for your own personal enjoyment and are reading it, please respect the hard work of this author and purchase a copy for yourself.

All rights reserved. No part of this book may be used or reproduced or transmitted in any manner whatsoever without written permission from the author, except for the inclusion of brief quotations in reviews, articles, and recommendations. Thank you for honoring this.

Illustrator: Mike Singh Bhangu
Published by BB Productions
British Columbia, Canada
crpublications@gmail.com

Table of Contents

Introduction

This manuscript stands on the premise that the person is built to be--built to be a patron of peace, a scholar of kindness, and an instrument of truth.

Introduction

Religions sometimes war, divide people, pit one against another, encourage murder, condone slavery, and sanction thievery. Using the three most affluent religions as a speaking point--Christianity, Judaism, and Islam, this manuscript explores why religions sometimes behave anti-God and several of the doctrinal inspirations.

The articles in this manuscript are from the book, *Secrets of Religion*. That book delves much deeper into the different religions and explains in more detail why religions stand on opposite ends. If you felt, *War and Religion*, was a valuable read, *Secrets of Religion* is sure to further provide you with golden nuggets.

Chasing Angels

I've unknowingly spent most of my life digging through religious riddles hidden underneath political truths. I've unknowingly spent most of my life shifting through the truths of religion and the truths of the Universe. And I've unknowingly spent most of my life, deaf and blind, chasing angels.

I've unknowingly spent because pieces of popular religions don't really make rational sense. For some reason, they create a divide between us, and us and the heavens--for instance, they readily hide the fact that there is truth in other religions. For some reason, religions support ideas that pit the likes of Jesus against the likes of Jesus--the thousands of Christian denominations are prime illustrations. And for some reason, they allowed self-interest to attribute untruths to the mouths of the God sent--for example, the Catholic Church tricked the masses to crusade by blurring the idea of salvation and sanctioning the act of murder in the name of Jesus[1], and the Islamic kingdoms of the past, such as the Ottoman Empire, used their faith to justify the slavery of other humans. The non-Muslims they didn't enslave were considered second-class citizens, as revealed by Robert Spencer, in his book, *The Politically Incorrect Guide to Islam and the Crusades* (Regnery Publishing: 2005), page 54.

But perhaps I'm mistaken and God truly did inspire the many divisions between religions, the many denominations within, and the many chains and bloodstained weapons. Maybe I'm mistaken and God truly did inspire evil things like the Catholic crusades,[2] the spiritual decimation of the First Nations,[3] the Spanish Inquisition,[4] Euro-centric motivations,[5] the attack on the Americans, the oppression of the Palestinians, slavery, doomsday predictions, and forceful conversions.

The Islamic Empire of the Mughals was the most infamous for such a practice. According to author, Max Arthur McAuliffe, in his book, *The Sikh Religion: Volume I*, the Mughals ruthlessly murdered hundreds of

7

thousands in their attempt to convert others to Islam. According to Sikh history and the stories found within Sikh literature, in their attempt to convert others to Islam, the Mughals employed heinous and ungodly measures. For example, they bricked alive two infant children on their refusal to accept the supremacy of Islam (the two youngest sons of Guru Gobind Singh), they executed two of India's greatest holy men because they were non-Muslim (Guru Arjan and Guru Tegh Bahadur), and they hunted all who belonged to the noble House of Nanak simply because they belonged to the House of Nanak. Nanak is the founder of Sikhism.

The Afghan Muslims, and obviously not all of them, behaved just as barbarically. They murdered en masse so to deny religious alternatives. In the year 1762, during one of their invasions into India, they annihilated twenty-thousand innocent Sikh women and children. They did horrible things such as throwing children into the air and spearing them as they fell, and snatching infants from their mothers, cutting them into pieces, and giving the remains back. The Afghan Muslims targeted women and children in an effort to deny the future of the Sikh faith.

History of the Origin and Progress of the Sikhs, written in 1778 by James Browne, tells that when the Afghan soldiers didn't murder, they would enslave non-Muslims--in particular, women. The women were typically sold into the sex trade or given to the soldiers.

John Malcolm, in his book, *Sketch of the Sikhs*, published in 1812, describes an instance when the Afghanies actually used the blood of slaughtered Sikhs to wash the walls of mosques. The Afghanies believed that the Sikhs polluted the mosques by entering them and the blood bath was meant to purify the buildings. (To learn more about the Sikh experience, please read, *Confessions: a lion's roar—a poet's war*).

Again, I could be wrong and God is truly concerned with control, power, and secular ambitions. Who knows, perhaps only some of us are God's children? God knows, that's exactly the message all popular religions seem to give and condition their followers into believing. For example, the most affluent religions of the world, Judaism, Christianity, and Islam, each claim that their doctrine is the only acceptable to God and no others. They also push the propaganda that, after the body falls, God will punish those who are not a member of their house. Jack Nelson-Pallmeyer, an expert on the topic, writes:

> "Jews claim to be God's chosen people, recipients of land, special promises, and noble mission. Christians say Jesus fulfilled Hebrew scriptural promises--a claim denied by Jews--that Jesus is the only way to God. The Quran is Allah's divinely inspired corrective to the errors propagated through the texts and conduct of Jews and Christians. It is the religious duty of Muslims to struggle (jihad) against unbelievers in order to establish a world in accord with Allah's intent."[6]

Not surprisingly, these three have killed each other for centuries in the name of God's Will.

What to make of all this, who is right and who is wrong? Could it be that they all hold truth? Could it be that they all harbour some degree of falsehood? And what explains the anti-God behaviour?

After taking the time to examine religions, it becomes apparent that they were infiltrated by selfish ambitions. What else explains the evil perpetrated under the banner of the Cross, the Star, and Islam? I've come to understand the pieces of doctrine that advocate or glorify murder, that depict God as violent, that use fear to gain obedience, that divide humanity, or that claim only a specific people are Godly as economic and political injections. Insertions designed by rulers to incite people to conquer others, to expand the boundaries of a nation or empire, to inspire and justify the brutish behaviour that always accompanies expansion, or to maintain the current state of affairs. They are not expressions of true religion.

Framed by the above stipulations, there appear to be religious ideas that are not inspired by The Great Architect and they've led to ungodly activities. The forthcoming pages provide several examples of that type of canon, and their design was inspired by the elite demographic, not the saintly, to maintain and enhance their power, and of course, to control the behaviour of the "bewildered herd".

This doesn't imply that political ambitions led to the establishment of religions. Most religions came before the politics and selfish people and groups eventually hijacked them. They astutely recognized religion as an instrument able to impress their will and increase their wealth. In addition, religion left to its own devices could threaten the power of those who rule, a lesson the early Christians taught the Roman Empire. When a religion does pose a threat to the establishment, the threatened will penetrate it and steer it away from them. In most cases, most religions came into existence as a challenge to the status quo, and by their nature, they were a threat to those who ruled.

Cunningly, after the incursion by selfish ambitions, ungodly doctrine strategically found its way among canon that emanates the aroma of Godliness. Godless dogma was placed amid the Godly so to give the appearance of a divine inspiration, and to manipulate the follower into believing it. Heavenly concepts are a part of all popular religion and they typically stress love, truth, compassion, humility, selflessness, unity, etc.

Celestial concepts are bundled with the opposite, and innocently, some people haven't thought enough about the origins and the history of religion to understand some of the politics, like those played by the Islamic Empires and the Roman Emperor Constantine.

Constantine decided to mix Pagan ideas from the Mithra tradition with Christian ideas, and unfortunately, some of the flock can't see the difference between the holy and the manmade--for example, they openly idolize the bones of dead saints.

Scholars suggest that Constantine, when he converted the Roman Empire from a Pagan Empire to a Christian Kingdom, behaved more as a politician than a Christian. Constantine allowed Pagan ideas such as idolizing bones to continue to exist so to appease the Pagan population. The symbol of the cross with a circle is another example of the marriage (it actually represents the Pagan Sun god), the idea of Trinity existed before Jesus but with different characters, and the Vatican is built on ancient Pagan spiritual land. Constantine's manipulation of the Christian dogma is given more attention in an impending article.

The same kind of political agenda is evident in Islam and it would seem that Godly ideas sit among doctrine that feels not so celestial. In the case of Islam, violent and oppressive passages were the outcome and nation building was the motivation. The atrocities committed by past Islamic Empires are the evidence. That said, Muslim scholars suggest that such kingdoms as the Mughal and Afghan Empires behaved more as Mongolians than they did Islamic. For that reason, they committed horrendous atrocities. Muslim scholars imply that true Islam doesn't sanction violence and conquest. They further suggest that the Mongols hijacked Islam on many fronts, distorted true Islam, and perpetuated a false Islam. As Christendom, Islam too was infiltrated long ago by greedy men and politicians. Muslim scholars believe popular Islam isn't what was conceptualized by Mohammad.

> *"(Remember) when your Lord inspired the angels, 'Verily, I am with you, so keep firm those who have believed. I will cast terror into the hearts of those who have disbelieved, so strike them over the necks, and smite over all their fingers and toes.'"*--(Qur'an 8:12)

> *"And when the sacred months have passed, then kill the polytheists wherever you find them and capture them and besiege them and sit in wait for them at every place of ambush. But if they should repent, establish prayer, and give*

zakah, let them [go] on their way. Indeed, Allah is Forgiving and Merciful."--(Qur'an 9:5)

After searching the contemporary Islamic doctrine, the case can be made that a few passages can be twisted to sanction violence. It's possible that the Muslim Empires would not have become so large if not for the sword and a hand to hold it--if not for doctrine able to rationalize the brutality of conquest. Or, for that matter, slave labour. The *Qur'an* makes several references to the subjugated.

"And marry those among you who are single and those who are fit among your male slaves and your female slaves..."-- (Qur'an 24:32)

"And if any of your slaves ask for a deed in writing (to enable them to earn their freedom for a certain sum), give them such a deed if you know any good in them; yes, give them something yourselves out of the means which Allah has given to you."--(Qur'an 24:33)

Although Islam permits slavery, by referring to it as a social norm, the *Qur'an* also suggests that it is righteous to free a slave.

"Righteousness is not that you turn your faces toward the east or the west, but [true] righteousness is [in] one who believes in Allah, the Last Day, the angels, the Book, and the prophets and gives wealth, in spite of love for it, to relatives, orphans, the needy, the traveler, those who ask [for help], and for freeing slaves..."--(Qur'an 2:177)

A contradiction is evident. To have slaves is acceptable but to free a slave is true righteousness. This is a prime example of the mix between Godly and ungodly canon.

The Prophet Mohammad existed and a celestial spark inspired his thoughts. After his birth, the world became a better place, as it did after the birth of people like Moses, Zoroaster, Buddha, Nanak, and Jesus. But as you'll discover in an upcoming article, Mohammad didn't write or compile the *Qur'an*. The creation of the *Qur'an* came after Mohammad ascended into "The White Light". Perhaps, if the *Qur'an* was finalized under his supervision, passages that create conflict and inspire slavery would not exist.

Islam isn't the only that accommodates the idea of oppressing another. Along with a superiority complex, as detailed in the upcoming articles, the Jewish doctrine too permits slavery.

> *"When Israel grew strong, they put the Canaanites to forced labor, but did not drive them out completely."*--(Judges 1:28)

> *"However, you may purchase male and female slaves from among the nations around you. You may also purchase the children of temporary residents who live among you, including those who have been born in your land. You may treat them as your property, passing them on to your children as a permanent inheritance. You may treat them as slaves, but you must never treat your fellow Israelites this way."*--(Leviticus 25:44–46)

And the Jewish doctrine also condemns the act. A contradiction there is.

> *"Whoever steals a man and sells him, and anyone found in possession of him, shall be put to death."*--(Exodus 21:16)

The inconsistencies exist because Godly ideas are presented with ideas not so Godly. The mix is the outcome of political and economic motivations. In the case of slavery, free labour is much more profitable than paying someone.

However, some people don't bother to question, and maybe, they're scared of the unknown and the mysterious muzzles their curiosity for reason. More important, no matter the scattered punctures, under the umbrella held by religion, it does feel safe and with purpose. The illusion can be enough to get through the everyday motions. But like every other, that artificial apparition will also fade and along with it the feelings it gives. One day, the circumstances will push us into the rain to search for God again.

I apologize if you find the ideas I'm presenting offensive. But please don't be mistaken. To temporarily sever the conditioned associations religions have instilled is not to separate the holy from the heavens. Nor is it a challenge aimed in that direction. It's an attempt to discover God again and to bring that truth back to every religion.

The excerpts used in this manuscript, from the different Holy Texts, are all translations and none of them were initially written in the English language. Misinterpretations and mistranslations are plausible.

God's People

> *"...It identifies the Israelites as God's chosen people, who, depending on which passages are cited, are destined by God either to be the vehicle through which God blesses all the nations, or to dominate the nations of the world. Most common are passages that confirm the latter view, with Isaiah's words being representative: Your gates shall always be open; day and night they shall not be shut, so that nations shall bring you their wealth, with their kings led in procession. For the nation and kingdom that will not serve you shall perish; those nations shall be utterly laid to waste. (60:11-12)"*--(Jack Nelson-Pallmeyer, *Is Religion Killing Us?: violence in the Bible and the Quran*, 2005, pg. 32)

The Jewish institution claims that they are the chosen people of God and no others. I think that idea was taught to the Jewish people to give them hope, confidence, self-respect, status, and strength to endure the hardship. From the philosopher's stone that I'm leaning on, all are the people of God and not just a specific group. To claim that one is more than another is to suggest that one is more than human.

The early history of the Jewish people is marked by hardship. They were persecuted and enslaved by the Babylonians, the Egyptians, the Greeks, and the Romans. Consequentially, the Jewish collective intelligence adopted a slave's mindset.

To break that mindset, it's plausible that the Jews were taught to believe they were God's people. A people can endure so much more when they believe that they're the chosen ones and their hardship has meaning. So much more can be achieved than through the mind of a slave.

It's also very possible that the Jewish people were given that notion so to persuade them to nation-build and to take another people's territory. The history of the Jewish institution, as depicted by the *Old Testament*, is extremely violent and on many occasions Biblical characters murdered and stole in God's Will, and in the end, to nation-build.

The Jewish institution is not alone in their claim that only they are the people of God. Islam also asserts the same.

"Truly, the religion with God is Islam."--(Qur'an 3:19)

Moreover, non-Muslims are labelled infidels (nonbelievers) and viewed as lesser because of their non-Islamic values. To give weight to that claim, elements of their doctrine can be twisted to suggest that it's the Will of God to subject the world's people to Islamic rule. Maybe, that's why the Islamic institutions were so deeply involved in the slave trade and able to morally justify caging other human beings like animals. Maybe, that's why the Islamic Empires, lost to the history books, readily murdered non-Muslims and took what was theirs. But again, the scholars suggest that the atrocities committed in the name of Islam were perpetuated by outsiders such as the Mongols, who hijacked Islam and changed it. And this argument makes sense. For what religion hasn't been usurped? In their purest manifestations, no religion sanctions senseless violence. Unfortunately, pure expressions of any religion are extremely difficult to locate.

"According to the founder and 'supreme guide' of the Muslim Brotherhood, Sheikh Hasan al-Banna, 'It is the nature of Islam to dominate, not to be dominated, to impose its law on all nations and to extend its power to the entire planet" (quoted in Taheri, 1987).[7]

Ayatollah Ruhollah Khomeini once said, *"Moslems have no alternative... to an armed holy war against profane governments....Holy war means the conquest of all non-Moslem territories....It will...be the duty of every able bodied adult male to volunteer for this war of conquest, the final aim of which is to put Koranic law in power from one end of the earth to the other.*"[8]

"And fight them until there is no more Fitnah (disbelief) and the religion will all be for Allah Alone."--(Qur'an 8:39)

"Fight against those who believe not in Allah, nor in the Last Day, nor forbid that which has been forbidden by Allah and His Messenger and those who acknowledge not the religion of truth (i.e. Islam) among the people of the Scripture (Jews and Christians), until they pay the Jizyah with willing submission, and feel themselves subdued."--(Qur'an 9:29)

"O you who believe! Fight those of the disbelievers who are close to you, and let them find harshness in you, and know that Allah is with those who are the Al-Muttaqun."--(Qur'an 9:123)

Under contemporary Islamic rule, non-Muslims can face three choices. Conversion to Islam, payment of a special tax (jizya), or death.[9]

Again, it's more than likely that Islam was hijacked, as Christianity was. For that reason, the Mohammedans were taught that Islam is the only path to God--to motivate large numbers of people to conquer their neighbours, to nation-build, and to justify the brutality that accompanies conquest. The Islamic Empires of the past, such as the Mughal and Afghan Empires, were not created through persuasion or love but more so by violence. Nor were they created in defense.[10] That's not to say Muslims can't live in harmony with people of other religions, they do and they have--typically, when radicalism isn't a nation's head and activating contradictory paragraphs. Even then, those who refuse to tolerate other faiths are few compared to the general public, and they do not pursue the passages in question. Nor are Muslims daily plotting to change the manner in which non-Muslims view life. Most of them overlook questionable canon and focus on the Godly ideas found within the *Qur'an.*

> *"Whoever saves the life of one human being, it shall be as if he had saved the whole of humankind"*--(Qur'an 5:32)

> *"Those who believe and do good deeds--the Gracious God will create love in their hearts."*--(Qur'an 19:97)

Through the use of propaganda designed to play with a person's loyalty to God, feelings such as fear, and the innate wants as outlined by Maslow in his Hierarchy of Needs, the political machine is what activates uncertain passages and misleads the believer to act on them. The political machine was also the force that inserted the questionable canon amongst Godly ideas in the first place. Secular motivations that even went as far as to oppress the female gender, when during Mohammad's time, women were regarded as equals.

The Hebrews and the Muslims are not the only people of God and the notions that suggest they are can only be political insertions designed to motivate the people to war and to conquer.

Godly messages were mixed with godless messages and presented as God sent, and unfortunately, the combination has existed for so long that it's evolved into a creature above rational debate. I'm sure that if a contest were to ensue, the reasonable person would conclude that it isn't the name of a religion that determines an individual's devotion but their state of awareness. God doesn't love religion. God loves the faithful.

In the end, every person has the right to harbour any belief they wish, but there is a difference between thoughts and actions.

Twisted Text

A large portion of the content within the different Holy Texts is God oriented. However, politically motivated insertions are plausible--injections easily twistable. These passages are few in relation to the entire content, but they're able to convince people to behave differently than the saintly would, and most horrific, to support war. Passages such as:

> *"Avenge the children of Israel of the Midianites: afterward shalt thou be gathered unto thy people."*--(Numbers 31:2)

> *"Think not that I am come to send peace on earth: I came not to send peace, but a sword."*--(Matthew 10:34)

> *"Give them according to their deeds, and according to the wickedness of their endeavours: give them after the work of their hands; render to them their desert."*--(Psalms 28:4)

> *"Or do you think that you will enter Paradise while Allah has not yet made evident those of you who fight in His cause and made evident those who are steadfast?"*--(Qur'an 3:142)

Who should determine whom to fight? Who should determine the causes prescribed by God? Who should determine what is evil and what is good? Those who determine can motivate the believers to any end they wish. For example, politicians can use the above passages to convince the flock to war against another nation. Politicians who do so will typically depict the nation they want to attack, or the governing body of that nation, as an evil. Then they'll link that evil to passages such as the above.

Passages can also be used to convince a people to ignore the harm one group might be causing another, by associating such things as war to the End of Days or to the Will of God.

"Then cometh the end, when he shall have delivered up the kingdom to God, even the Father; when he shall have put down all rule and all authority and power."--(Corinthians 15:24)

"Say to those with fearful hearts, "Be strong, do not fear; your God will come, he will come with vengeance; with divine retribution he will come to save you."--(Isaiah 35:4)

"The four angels were released, who had been held ready for the hour, the day, the month, and the year, to kill a third of humankind."--(Rev 9:15)

"And the armies which are in heaven, clothed in fine linen, white and clean, were following Him on white horses. From His mouth comes a sharp sword, so that with it He may strike down the nations, and He will rule them with a rod of iron; and He treads the wine press of the fierce wrath of God, the Almighty. And on His robe and on His thigh He has a name written, 'KING OF KINGS, AND LORD OF LORDS.'"--(Rev 14-16)

"The angel swung his sickle on the earth, gathered its grapes and threw them into the great winepress of God's wrath."--(Rev 14:19)

"Fighting is prescribed for you, and ye dislike it. But it is possible that ye dislike a thing which is good for you, and that ye love a thing which is bad for you. But Allah knoweth, and ye know not."--(Qur'an 2:216)

The majority of the content within the Holy Texts is God oriented. Every person should study the Text(s) of their religion. A better understanding of The Great Architect will be the outcome. However, politically motivated insertions are evident. These passages are few in comparison to the entire content, but they're able to convince a person to behave anti-God.

The believer has little choice but to employ the art of critical thought when passages from a Holy Text are used to convince people to behave less than a child of God. Without critical thought, a person might accidentally subject the self to negative celestial consequence.

"You have heard that it was said, 'Love your neighbor and hate your enemy.' But I tell you, love your enemies and pray for those who persecute you, that you may be children of your Father in heaven. He causes his sun to rise on the evil and the good, and sends rain on the righteous and the unrighteous."--(Matthew 5:43-45)

God's People II

Regardless of how popular media presents it, the state of Israel sometimes behaves like those who attack them, and the fact of the matter is, after the Second World War, the United States, France, and Britain created the nation-state of Israel. In doing so, they immorally removed the Palestinians from parts of their homeland.

Even after the 1979 peace treaty between Israel and Palestine, in which the two sides agreed to a border and a cease-fire, Israel continued to take. That said; it could be that Israel continued to increase her size so to create a buffer zone between Israel and the terrorists who just won't stop attacking innocent Israelis. But, in doing so, and according to Sufyan Omeish and Abdallah Omeish in their video documentary, *Occupation 101: Voices of the Silenced Majority* (2006), Israel is illegally and unjustly invading and colonizing Palestinian land. In the process, Israel is forcefully removing Palestinians from their homes.

Imagine if that was happening where you live. What would you do if another people decided to use their military strength to remove you from your home and occupy your land?

Jimmy Carter, former President of the United States, in his book, *Palestine: Peace Not Apartheid* (2006), compares the Israeli Government to the apartheid government that once existed in South Africa.

Even some Israeli soldiers disagree with the occupation of Palestine-- they think Israel is acting immorally (Journeyman Pictures, *Crisis of Conscience--Israel/Palestine*, 2002).

However, mainstream media doesn't present the Palestinian plight as righteous. Instead, they sometimes create a similar atmosphere to the "Two Minutes Hate" ritual in the novel, *1984*, by George Orwell. In that, they hide the innocent Palestinian faces killed in the madness and more so highlight the crazed Islamic terrorists.

It would seem that when they talk about peace in the Mid-East, what they're actually talking about is creating an environment where Israel can peacefully take away Palestinian land.

I can't help but feel that those Jewish people willing to invade, occupy, oppress, displace other human beings, or generate terror were inspired or desensitized by the scattered darkness found within the *Old Testament*, and by the idea that they are the people of God and no others are. They're trapped in an Iron Cage similar to what Max Weber once described and to ideas that can only be political injections. Political insertions designed to motivate a group of people to nation build, to feel comfortable with the atrocities spurred in the process, and to desensitize them to violence. Passages such as:

> *" 'Go up against the land of Merathaim, and against the inhabitants of Pekod. Kill, and devote them to destruction, declares the LORD, and do all that I have commanded you.' "*--(Jeremiah 50:21)

> *"And while the children of Israel were in the wilderness, they found a man that gathered sticks upon the sabbath day. And they that found him gathering sticks brought him unto Moses and Aaron, and unto all the congregation. And they put him in ward, because it was not declared what should be done to him. And the Lord said unto Moses, The man shall be surely put to death: all the congregation shall stone him with stones without the camp. And all the congregation brought him without the camp, and stoned him with stones, and he died; as the Lord commanded Moses."*--(Numbers 15:32-36)

> *"When you march up to attack a city, make its people an offer of peace. If they accept and open their gates, all the people in it shall be subject to forced labour (slavery) and*

shall work for you. If they refuse to make peace and they engage you in battle, lay siege to that city. When the Lord your God delivers it into your hand, put to the sword all the men in it. As for the women, the children, the livestock and everything else in the city, you may take these as plunder for yourselves. And you may use the plunder the Lord your God gives you from your enemies. This is how you are to treat all the cities that are at a distance from you and do not belong to the nations nearby. However, in the cities of the nations the Lord your God is giving you as an inheritance, do not leave alive anything that breathes. Completely destroy them--the Hittites, Amorites, Canaanites, Perizzites, Hivites and Jebusites--as the Lord your God has commanded you. Otherwise, they will teach you to follow all the detestable things they do in worshiping their gods, and you will sin against the Lord your God."--
(Deuteronomy 20:10-18)

Concepts that contradict violent behaviour can also be found within the Hebrew faith and they are more in number than the questionable canon. But during times of conquest, they're abandoned by the political machine and more so remembered when there is no application required.

"When a stranger sojourns with you in your land, you shall not do him wrong. You shall treat the stranger who sojourns with you as the native among you, and you shall love him as yourself, for you were strangers in the land of Egypt: I am the LORD your God."--(Leviticus 19:33-34)

The events in the Middle-East are contemporary examples of the impact violent doctrine can have. No matter if the passages constitute only a tiny percentage of the overall message. The events are also an excellent example of the political influence over dogma.

The political manipulation has convinced the people of Israel that they have some sort of Divine right to the land there. Passages such as *Genesis 12:7* and *Genesis 15:18* are readily asserted. The supposed Godly passages appear to sanction the displacement and murder of the Palestinians.

Murder isn't the only anti-God element within the Jewish literature, as pointed to in a previous article, slavery is accepted by Jewish doctrine-- complimented by an attitude of superiority. For example:

> *"Rab Judah said in the name of Samuel: The property of a heathen (non-Jewish) is on the same footing as desert land; whoever first occupies it acquires ownership."*--(Babylonian Talmud: Baba Bathra, Folio 54b)

> *"'Where a suit arises between an Israelite and a heathen (non-Jewish), if you can justify the former according to the laws of Israel, justify him and say: 'This is our law'; so also if you can justify him by the laws of the heathens justify him and say [to the other party:] 'This is your law'; but if this cannot be done, we use subterfuges (deceptions) to circumvent him."*--(Babylonian Talmud: Baba Kamma, Folio 113a)

As in the case of Islam, not all the Hebrews value dark affirmations, but there are enough in positions of power to nullify the beliefs of the majority.

It is suggested that the political system, Zionism, is responsible for the carnage and not the Jewish people. There is a division of society in the state of Israel, between the rulers and the ruled. The latter, as in every nation and religion, are typically innocent victims of the selfish economic and political objectives of the former.

Eco-political intentions not only trick the innocent people of Israel, Christendom too is convinced of Israel's heavenly right to occupy the

Palestinian. Specifically, the Christians who believe the Jewish people are the chosen people. Christian nations such as America donate billions of dollars to Israel, and Christians from around the world have also relocated to Israel to occupy lands taken from the Palestinians. There aren't enough Israelis to settle the stolen territory, and without a human presence, it's difficult to keep what's annexed--a fundamental understanding when attempting to build a nation. Like pawns, the people of Jesus are treated, but tragically, they believe differently. They believe they're fulfilling a holy mission.

Oddly, the idea of the Jewish people as God's people doesn't include the Christians. They're in the same boat as the rest of the people of the planet.

In the beginning, Britain, France, and America instigated the troubles between Palestine and Israel, and so much drama has taken place between the two that the idea of the freedom-fighter and the terrorist is sometimes blurred. I think it's safe to say that all sides shelter both the terms. The Palestinians and the Israelis have both played the role of the terrorist. However, I think it's time that the Palestinians recognize the nation-state of Israel. Israel has a right to exist and they aren't going anywhere. But unfortunately, terror groups such as Hamas are misleading the Palestinian people, and Hamas does not desire peace. Surprisingly, Hamas will even kill fellow Palestinians if they behave outside Islamic notions. Hamas is completely barbaric--I've seen video footage of them shooting people for simply dancing. I also think that Israel should contribute to the peace process and cease her expansionist policy. Perhaps, if the two sides change their attitudes, peace in the Middle-East can be a reality.

End of Days

Some groups twisted the passages in their Text and convinced the faithful to Jihad. They forgot that the murder of the innocent accompanies negative celestial consequence and not a flock of virgins.

Some groups twisted the passages in their Text and now people wail against a wall to please The Formless. They idolize as if they forgot the magnificent Moses.

Some groups twisted the passages in their Text and subjugated the female. They oppressed the gender who gave the world the likes of Nanak, Buddha, Mohammad, and Jesus.

Some groups twisted the passages in their Text and turned a faithful into a prostitute (Mary Magdalene).[11] They attempt to rob the human potential.

Some groups twisted the passages in their Text and made hatred holy. They justified racism and the enslavement of the African[12] by suggesting, for example, the mark of Cain, discussed in *Genesis 4*, is the reason the Africans are dark-skinned. The Africans were depicted as the descendents of the evil Cain, and because they were, their enslavement was sanctioned. I guess the haters were oblivious to the fact that the face of Jesus was also painted.

Some groups twisted the passages in their Text and now act as if global warming is an indication of the end and a Godly phenomenon. They ignore the fact that the effect is manmade and humanity has the power to reverse the damage they've done. They, instead of protecting our First Mother, protect those who pollute and plunder. They do that by pretending the damage large corporations do to the planet, in their search for more profit, is an act of The Eternal.

And some groups twisted the passages in their Text and persuaded their congregation that God is hell-bent. They comically wait in excited anticipation for the days to end. More than 2 millennia have passed and some are still under the impression that the end of days will come tomorrow or the next.[13] Similar in comparison to when most thought that the earth was flat--people are misled but assume they're on the right track. Ironically, almost every generation has a group who thinks their generation will be the last, and they all point to the negative world events of their time as the indicators of the end.[14]

But even more shocking, there are actually some who work to bring forth the Apocalypse, or what the Hebrews call "the Eschaton", like Captain Ahab chased Moby Dick. Although the majority of the people who believe in Judgment Day aren't obsessed with bringing it forth, there are those, categorized as "activists", who actively seek to bring about the end.[15] Intoxicated by the illusion of a heavenly will,[16] they plot, scheme, and fuel wars to create the circumstances and material things necessary to usher in the Day of Judgment. Circumstances as the complete occupation of the "Promised Land" by the Jewish people,[17] and material things as the Temple of Solomon.[18]

Coincidentally, half of the "Promised Land" is home to Muslims (the Palestinians), and the place where the fundamentalists have indicated that the Temple of Solomon must be is the exact place where the Temple Mount is. The Temple Mount is one of the holiest sites in Islam. Can you see the problem? But bloodshed is anticipated by the seekers of Apocalypse.[19] They fully accept that millions must die for them to live in the Kingdom of Heaven. They fully believe that mass murder is a precursor to their happiness--readily disguising it as a battle against evil and the "Will" of God.[20]

The activists aren't satisfied with God's timeline, and instead, they believe they can provoke God into acting.

I'm sure there will be an end to humanity. Everything that has a beginning has an end (excluding The Eternal). But that end time is not for humanity to determine. When God is ready to end humanity, I'm sure God will, and since The Formless is infinitely stronger than every person combined together is, I don't think God would need mere mortals to carry out the plan. As for the Kingdom of Heaven, take a read at what Jesus had to say about the topic.

> *"His disciples said to Him, 'When will the repose of the dead come about, and when will the new world come?' He said to them, 'What you look forward to has already come, but you do not recognize it.'"*--(Gospel of Thomas)

Luke further explains:

> *"And when he was demanded of the Pharisees, when the kingdom of God should come, he answered them and said, The kingdom of God cometh not with observation: Neither shall they say, Lo here! or, lo there! for, behold, the kingdom of God is within you."*--(Luke 17:20-21)

I ask--is doctrine so easily twisted actually the ideas and words of God as each believes, or were they political insertions placed amongst Godly doctrine and taught as truth to deceive?

> *"Cruel men believe in a cruel God and use their belief to excuse their cruelty. Only kindly men believe in a kindly God, and they would be kindly in any case."*--Bertrand Russell (1953)

In Search of God

A person will search for God when times are tough. But when times are tough, a person is typically weak in mind and susceptible. In such a state, a person will move toward what's easily available, and a person will most likely believe almost anyone who gives even a glimpse of hope. Tell me, what else explains the religious suicide cults like Heaven's Gate, Jonestown, and the Order of the Solar Temple? What else explains the door-to-door bible thumper?

On the latter, they believe that they're doing the work of God by attempting to increase their denomination's membership. They fail to recognize that they're actually working on behalf of the denomination's administration to increase donations and fatten their pockets.

The denominations that do encourage door-to-door thumping typically send the innocent. Based on my observations, it would appear that they send out the members who look most innocent and trustworthy like elderly women and young children. They exploit innocence like the media exploits promiscuity.

My viewpoint of the door-to-door bible thumper is based on my observations of "the doom" group known as the Jehovah's Witnesses, and they're one of many who like to push the propaganda that the world is about to end.

This *Scripture*-inspired denomination of Christianity has been in the business of prophesising for over a century, and "doomsday" is the reason they came to be. According to author, James Penton, in his book, *Apocalypse Delayed: the story of Jehovah's Witnesses* (1985), originally, they believed that Jesus Christ, in 1874, came again in his second invisible presence and the world would end in 1914 with Jesus Christ as the Supreme Authority of all world governments. When 1914 came and went, they predicted a new date, 1915, and when 1915 came and went, another date was predicted, 1918. Again, when that date was proven inaccurate, Jerry L. Walls tells us, in his book, *The Oxford Handbook of Eschatology* (2007), a new date was set for the beginning of the end of days, 1925. Not surprisingly, that date too came and went. But surprisingly, some Jehovah's Witnesses still continue to fall for the propaganda that Armageddon is just around the bend. Them are easily exploited and this religious institution readily twists the Text to suit an end-of-days prediction.

I have to say, the Jehovah's Witnesses do attempt to live a life governed by the better half of the mind, and it's not the follower I'm wondering about, for they are God seekers, it's the institution that is Jehovah's Witnesses and their willingness to exploit and scare the person that troubles me.

A person will search for God when times are tough. However, when times are tough, a person is usually weak in mind and susceptible, and some religions behave like predators.

Elysian

There exists God inspired dogma and there exists doctrine that doesn't have the same feel. The Godly inspires an aura of peace and harmony within and the opposite inspires an aura of discomfort. I do not question the doctrine that brings peace and harmony to the "I" in me, but I can't help but question dogma that doesn't.

I can't help but question because only in truth is there salvation for the soul. For if I misinterpret the Universal principles that govern life and death, the "truest me" might not progress and advance like the "truest me" was meant to.

Like a caterpillar without the cocoon. Like a seed that wasn't sowed. Like a fool that threw away a gift from The Eternal.

Godly ideas are in every religion, and it is to them a person should give their allegiance. All ideas outside of them, no matter the paragraph before and after, are political creations.

Fortunate for religion but unfortunate for the woman and man, every generation is born unaware of what is and what was, and generations born to tomorrow won't know of the past if the past isn't taught.

The Pretender

Ignorant is thee who pretends to be. Separate they be from the better half in thee. Blind in mind they breathe and daily repeat. I speak of those who carry the name and symbols without the understanding.

An example of a pretender is a person who bares the symbols of a religion but terrorizes the innocent. Or a person who raps about The One Virtuous Lord in the same verse in which ungodly thoughts and behaviour are dancing.

We've all witnessed the pretenders and no religion is without the black marks. There isn't a religion in the world that the Age of Darkness didn't infiltrate.

The Age of Darkness, also known as the Age of Iron, has infiltrated religions and the pretender is a manifestation. With little knowledge of their faith's philosophy and narration, they carry the name as if it was a part of their disposition. In the process, they give a distorted definition.

Tragically, the distortion is wrongly influencing the newer generations, and the misdirection has wrongly given the outsiders looking in an inaccurate definition. Regrettably, the result has been a further alienation from the likes of the God sent and the truth in their religions.

A faith is not a birthright. It is to be or not to be. All faiths are holy. It's a matter of being.

Age of Darkness

According to Eastern religious philosophy, the world continuously cycles through four ages, and each era produces a different type of civilization, as determined by the distance between humanity and God. In the first age, the people are closest to God and there exists only one religion. All people have God knowledge and all people are wardens of a God-Consciousness. But with each proceeding age, the people regress and move further from God, God knowledge, and a God-Consciousness. According to Sikh teachings, humanity is currently in the fourth era, the Age of Kali Yuga.

The forth epoch is said to be the darkest of all and furthest from the era of perfect existence. It is a time of dark influences and home to untruths. To one degree or another, almost all institutions facilitate falsehoods. That includes the culture and the intelligence filled and shaped by those institutions, and every person who makes contact with them. Furthermore, the universe is predisposed to sway a person's consciousness to favour the five thieves over the five weapons.

The four ages are: The Golden Age of Sat Yuga, the Silver Age of Trayta Yuga (Ram existed in this era), the Brass Age of Dwaapar Yuga (Krishna existed in this era), and the Iron Age of Kali Yuga (also called the Age of Darkness).

"In the Golden Age of Sat Yuga, everyone embodied contentment and meditation; religion stood upon four feet. With mind and body, they sang of the Lord, and attained supreme peace. In their hearts was the spiritual wisdom of the Lord's Glorious Virtues. Their wealth was the spiritual wisdom of the Lord's Glorious Virtues; the Lord was their success, and to live as Gurmukh was their glory. Inwardly and outwardly, they saw only the One Lord God; for them there was no other second. They centered their consciousness lovingly on the Lord, Har, Har. The Lord's

Name was their companion, and in the Court of the Lord, they obtained honor. In the Golden Age of Sat Yuga, everyone embodied contentment and meditation; religion stood upon four feet. || 1 || Then came the Silver Age of Trayta Yuga; men's minds were ruled by power, and they practiced celibacy and self-discipline. The fourth foot of religion dropped off, and three remained. Their hearts and minds were inflamed with anger. Their hearts and minds were filled with the horribly poisonous essence of anger. The kings fought their wars and obtained only pain. Their minds were afflicted with the illness of egotism, and their self-conceit and arrogance increased. If my Lord, Har, Har, shows His Mercy, my Lord and Master eradicates the poison by the Guru's Teachings and the Lord's Name. Then came the Silver Age of Trayta Yuga; men's minds were ruled by power, and they practiced celibacy and self-discipline. || 2 || The Brass Age of Dwaapar Yuga came, and people wandered in doubt. The Lord created the Gopis and Krishna. The penitents practiced penance, they offered sacred feasts and charity, and performed many rituals and religious rites. They performed many rituals and religious rites; two legs of religion dropped away, and only two legs remained. So many heroes waged great wars; in their egos they were ruined, and they ruined others as well. The Lord, Compassionate to the poor, led them to meet the Holy Guru. Meeting the True Guru, their filth is washed away. The Brass Age of Dwaapar Yuga came, and the people wandered in doubt. The Lord created the Gopis and Krishna. || 3 || The Lord ushered in the Dark Age, the Iron Age of Kali Yuga; three legs of religion were lost, and only the fourth leg remained intact. Acting in accordance with the Word of the Guru's Shabad, the medicine of the Lord's Name is obtained. Singing the Kirtan of the Lord's Praises, divine peace is obtained. The season of singing the Lord's Praise has arrived; the Lord's Name is glorified, and the Name of the Lord, Har, Har, grows in the field of the body. In the Dark Age of Kali Yuga, if one plants any other seed than the Name, all profit and capital is lost. Servant Nanak has found the Perfect Guru, who has revealed to him the Naam within his heart and mind. The Lord ushered in the Dark Age, the Iron Age of Kali Yuga; three legs of religion were lost, and only the fourth leg remained intact. || 4 || 4 || 11 ||"--(Sri Guru Granth Sahib Ji, ang 445-446 of 1430)

The term "Guru", used in the above passage, refers to God's Spirit and not a person. The name "Har, Har" is a name used to describe God. The Sikh Holy Text uses many different names to reference God.

This idea of the four ages is not exclusive to Sikhie thought and it's a very ancient idea that predates the oldest literature in the world, the Vedic literature. (If you would like to learn more about the Sikh people or the Sikh philosophy, please read *Sikhie Secrets* and *Confessions: a lion's roar—a poet's war*).

Set to last approximately 24 000 years, there are two theories to what happens after this age. One suggests that the cycle starts again with Sat Yuga. Another theory suggests that the cycle doesn't begin again with Sat Yuga but instead descends after Kali Yuga passes.

The ancient Egyptians, Greeks, Mayans, and Romans too valued this idea of the different epochs, with Greek philosophy hosting an additional age, the Age of Heroes. They even possessed maps of a world before the transition to the current age. On those maps, Antarctica isn't covered by ice and the above sea land mass is much larger. The Piri Reis Map and the Oronteus Finaeus Map, among others, are said to originate from those ancient maps.

Interestingly, the theory of the four ages provides an answer to a question mainstream historians are troubled by. They don't know or don't believe how the early civilizations, such as the Egyptians, gained the knowledge that allowed them to spontaneously civilize. They've even gone as far as to suggest that aliens were responsible for their advancement. But according to the ancient Egyptians, the knowledge required to civilize came from the previous ages, and it was knowledge that survived the transition from one era to another. The Sphinx is said to be from the previous age. Geologists have determined that the Sphinx is actually older than 10 000 years. They've determined that by examining the weathering the Sphinx has experienced. The examination determined that at one point, the Sphinx was exposed to rain, and the Sahara hasn't experienced a rainfall in over 10 000 years. If this is true, then the civilizations of this age are not as advanced as the civilizations of the past. We're playing catch-up. The supposition reminds me of a particular idea found in the Christian doctrine:

> "What has been is what will be, and what has been done is what will be done; there is nothing new under the sun."-- (Ecclesiastes 1:4-11)

It should be mentioned that before the introduction of each of the four eras, and before an age begins a decline, there happens a large-scale catastrophic event such as a deluge that erases the majority of a civilization (people, culture, architecture, knowledge, technology, etc). Catastrophic world events take place before the introduction of an era to wipe clear what is. Each era gives birth to a new type of civilization, and for the new to fully be, in this case, the old must first be near-erased. The Mayans believed that human civilizations have been wiped-out five times already. Ancient cultures from around the world also claim that civilizations were annihilated. For example, the Sumer story of Ziusudra, the Indian story of Manu, the Greek story of Deucalion, the Babylonian story of Utnapishtim, and the Hebrew story of Noah all describe civilization-destroying catastrophes.

In each age, the alignment of the planets is different from the others, and it's the change in the arrangement of the planets that stimulates catastrophic world events. In the Age of Sat Yug, in relation to the earth, Venus and Saturn play a much more dominant role. The symbol of Islam reflects that idea. Supposedly, the symbol is not of the Moon and Sun, but of Venus and Saturn.

Other mysteries are also put into perspective when the theory of the four ages is applied to them. For example, the questions surrounding some of the megalithic structures found all over the world become less when considering the eras. It's possible that they were designed the sizes they were, in a previous age, to survive catastrophic world events brought forth by the transition from one epoch to another. Perhaps, the heavens inspired as they motivated Noah, but instead of a boat, instructions were provided to build huge stone structures.

Whereas ships such as Noah's stored life, the megalithic structures of the world might be designed to give knowledge. They just have to be looked at in the right light. For example, they give accurate astrological readings, their proportions are precise and mathematically arranged, they exhibit signs that advanced technology was used to make them, and they're built on what the Chinese call dragon lines (earth energy lines). It's also possible they were designed to store written knowledge in the form of books and such, and that knowledge was retrieved after a catastrophic event. Perhaps, a storehouse of knowledge is yet to be recovered.

Ships and megalithic buildings are not the only type of structures supposedly inspired by the heavens to survive an upcoming natural disaster. For example, in the second chapter of the *Vendidad*, a division of the Zoroastrian holy book *Avesta,* God warned the Persian King Yima, the son of Vivanghat, of an upcoming natural disaster. God further instructed him to build underground cities and take shelter. Derinkuyu, the massive underground city discovered in Turkey, which can house as many as twenty thousand people and the required livestock, is said to be one of the cities Yima built.

Elaborate underground cities, complexes, and tunnel systems are not all that strange. The ancient cultures from all over the world have one story or another detailing such things. For example, the Hopi and the Apache Indians believe that their ancestors once lived underground, and only after a great calamity, did they resurface.

In his book, *Weird America*, Jim Brandon shares the legend of the city underneath California's Death Valley called "Shin-Au-Av". The story originates from the Paiute Indians, and supposedly, in this mysterious underground complex, once lived an unknown race of people. The Sioux Indians also share an underground city story, in which one of their people, White Horse, accidentally found an underground city occupied by strange humans. These underground humans gave White Horse a mystical talisman capable of melting rocks.

There are numerous stories from all over the world detailing the existence of underground cities, complexes, and tunnels. The two most famous hidden underground cities are Agartha and Shambhala, with the supposed entrance to the first at the South Pole. Nazi Germany is said to have spent enormous amounts of money looking for the two, and it's suggested that they actually found Agharta. There, live tall, blonde, and blue-eyed people.

According to Eastern religious philosophy, the world continuously cycles through four ages and humanity is currently in the fourth, the Age of Iron.

The New Testament too expresses the idea of Ages, but the notion was lost in translation, and the following passage is plausibly inaccurate.

> *"Teaching them to observe all things whatsoever I have commanded you: and, lo, I am with you always, even unto the end of the world. Amen."*--(Matthew 28:20)

In Greek, the word in the above passage translated as "world" is mistranslated, and if correctly translated, the word would be "aeon". So, the passage should read:

> *"Teaching them to observe all things whatsoever I have commanded you: and, lo, I am with you always, even unto the end of the aeon. Amen."*--(Matthew 28:20)

The mistranslations in the New Testament limit the Christian understanding of the Universe, and because of the above mistranslation, the Christian world, who read the English version of the New Testament, see the end of this Epoch as the end of human existence--the end days. However, the end of this Age is not the end of humanity, and it is only the end of this type of human living and being.

Playing With Iron

Humanity is currently in the midst of the Iron Age. In this era, it is said that every institution built by man will eventually corrupt - regardless if the intention behind the creation is benevolent.

Some corrupt within a generation and others in several more. No government, religion, non-profit organization, or corporation is sheltered from the shadows, and no amount of earthly currency can buy protection from the Age of Iron.

The Dark Side of the Church

For the days now gone, blame the generations who betrayed our innocence. Blame those who muddied religion that now fools the innocent.

It's more than evident that the truths proclaimed by some can't be trusted, and they can't be trusted because a selfish agenda motivated some to purposely corrupt them. The past British Empire is one of the biggest culprits. They're responsible for distorting historical and cultural knowledge and injecting lies into the Empire's collective intelligence.[21] The British Empire did that to gain popular support for imperialism and to control what wasn't theirs to have. In the process, they corrupted the heritage of the world and polluted the minds of those who encountered them.

For example, with the rise of European colonialism and imperialism, the European decision-makers purposely injected untruthful information into their respective European cultures. That information depicted the coloured people of the world as intellectually and morally inferior. They injected that type of information so to garnish their colonial and imperial motivations as acts of liberation and divine purpose, and to help their populace feel comfortable with the evil that accompanies occupation and exploitation.

Sometimes the colonialists ignored, sometimes they labelled, and sometimes they attempted to change what is. For example, when an interest in ancient Egypt first surfaced, the Europeans completely ignored the fact that there were once powerful Black Pharaohs in Egypt--instead, they were depicted as light skinned. Europe makes the claim that the printing press and the compass are European innovations but the Chinese actually invented them. And the contemporary Western World credits the ancient Greek philosophers as the pioneers of thought but the fact remains that the Persian and the Indian philosophers came centuries before the likes of Aristotle. In actuality, the Greeks referenced them, including the greats such as Pythagoras, Socrates, and Zeno. The foundation of Western culture is not Greco-Roman but Indo-Persian.

Opportune for them, but tragic for the woman and man, the person is born unaware of the truth. Moreover, the human is born innocent and will trust almost all information presented as honest. As such, it's nearly impossible to know what isn't shown without digging through all the political rhetoric, the selfish insertions, and the out and out false information presented as honest.

To that end, some in the contemporary Western World do not see the British colonial era through the same prescription glasses, and the lenses they wear keep their vision slightly out of focus. What I'm suggesting is that the majority of the population were shown only the positive elements such as early industrialization, and they were given an inaccurate image that depicted the occupied as a morally, spiritually, economically, and intellectually inferior people. Needless to say, the British employed the language of deliberate deception and most people under their influence were victims of misinformation.

One of the most popular lies the British-history books like to propagate is that the British Empire was benevolent and that's why they grew to be a world power. Unfortunately, the reality is much different. The British Empire reached the size it did because they destroyed people, local economies, customs, history, and righteous cultures in an attempt to fulfill their imperial agenda. There is no question that they employed deceit as if they were the shadows of the devil. Their demonic tactics are what allowed them to occupy other people.

For example, they would enter the territory that interested their imperial agenda and befriend the people of that nation, under the guise of friendship, honesty, truth, and mutual cooperation, they would learn the manner in which the leadership governed their people, the local culture, and the existing conflicts that divided the people. After which, they would network with those opposed to the governing body. When the opportunity presented itself, the British would use their knowledge to topple the governing body and then replace it with a body they could control. They would then enslave the locals and sully their economy, culture, political makeup, and spiritual customs. In addition, they murdered the unsuspecting on mass and pitted people against people if required to maintain their power.

During the time of colonialism, the language of deliberate deception was employed to garnish domestic support. Without support from the populace, the Crown could not wage war and occupy other nations and people. If the domestic populace knew that the British Empire was slaying noble and just people who were of a noble and just society, the people of England would've risen up against such an ungodly endeavour. But they were misled to believe that the British were saving the people of the world from themselves and introducing superior moral, spiritual, economic, and intellectual principles rather than annihilating them. It's much easier to support conquest if the general population of the invader believe they're acting for the good of humanity. More so if they believe they're acting on behalf of God--an idea that was also conditioned and readily reinforced to motivate the people to overlook and even undertake ungodly acts.

Unfortunately, the British weren't the only culprits. Throughout the recorded centuries, many nations, religions, groups, and institutions the world over did the same. Another good example, on par with British colonialism, is the offspring of the Roman Empire, the Catholic Church.[22]

Based on historical accounts, the Roman Empire didn't fall but slowly transitioned into what is now the Catholic Church. After that, the Church used the language of deliberate deception, just as the British Empire did, to foster ideas that benefit the rulers and create an illusion. In the process, they readily behaved differently than Jesus did. For example, the Church:

1) Burned people on the stake... the Inquisitions. Countless innocent people were eliminated.

2) Deemed the woman as inferior and not equal... *"St. Paul, in the first epistle to the Corinthians, condemns woman's participation in the exercises of worship and instruction in the Christian assemblies of Corinth."*[23]

3) Persecuted the likes of Galileo for proclaiming that the earth didn't stand still and wasn't the center of the Universe.[24] They further convinced countless people that the third planet from the sun was flat and man could fall off the edge. Along with an inaccurate theory that suggests the formation of the planet happened 6000 years in the past.[25]

Under the watch of the Church, to keep the general public ignorant, knowledge was distorted. Knowledge is power and the Church, like the other religious institutions, isn't in the business of empowering their followers. Religions are instruments of the rulers to herd the ruled. Just like the institution of government sometimes is.

4) Openly attacked the Jewish people by proclaiming that they killed Jesus, and the Church used passages from *Scripture* to do it. Statements such as the one made by the Roman Procurator, Pontius Pilate, as he was washing his hands before a crowd of Jewish people who were calling for the death of the Saviour: *"I am innocent of this man's blood; see to it yourselves."*[26]

5) Murdered other Christians such as the noble Gnostics and Cathars.[27] The Church did that to consolidate their power as the only institution of Jesus. Groups such as the Cathars were openly denying the divine authority of the Pope, and teaching a doctrine faithful to the *Scriptures*-- propositions that threatened the power of the Church.

Before, during, and after the killing of all competing groups, the Church branded them as an evil. Seventeen-hundred years later and still those groups are remembered as the devil's minions.

The Church typically labels most other religious groups able to threaten their power as anti-God, and the Church is known to discredit knowledge that could empower a person. An empowered individual has little need for an intermediary establishment, and an empowered person has the potential to challenge the authority of the rulers. It would be reasonable to examine the knowledge they discredit and determine the value of it for the self.

The Catholic Church isn't the only entity that attacked knowledge able to liberate a person, and all ruling parties from all over the world did the same. The storehouses of wisdom such as the Library of Alexandria, the magnificent Library of Nalanda, the Mayan libraries of the Yucatan, the Library of Al-Hakam II, the Xianyang Palace Library, the American Library of Congress in 1814, and the Sikh Reference Library in 1984 were destroyed for that reason.

However, when it isn't possible to eradicate knowledge, the powerful will infiltrate the institution built to communicate that knowledge, and from within they will manipulate the information delivered to the general public--concealing the knowledge able to enhance a person's awareness of the self and the world. Furthermore, they will popularize information designed to misdirect the truth seeker.

6) Denied all knowledge of Jesus and Christianity that they themselves didn't package and cater, for example:

a. It's more than plausible that Jesus Christ traveled to India during his missing years[28] but the Church can't accept the possibility that Jesus mingled with Indian holy men.

b. The evidence suggests that Jesus wasn't born on December 25th but the Catholic Church ignores the data. The Church ignores the suggestion because if the Church acknowledges the possibility the Church will be revealed as fallible and not so divine.

The evidence hints that the date December 25th was given by the Roman Empire to appease the Pagan population and their sun god, at a time when Christianity was still young and looking for converts.[29] That said, the date of his birth doesn't truly matter. It's his life that should be remembered. Focus your consciousness on the Christ Consciousness every day and not just on a particular day or month.

    c. Destroyed dozens of competing Christian *Gospels* after the creation of the *New Testament*.

7) Assisted Hitler's henchmen during World War II, and factions of the Church helped several Nazis escape post-war judgement.[30]

8) Forcefully converted the First Nations people to Catholicism so they could be used as a subservient labour pool. The Catholic Residential Schools built to achieve that end are remembered by the First Nations people as places of torture, murder, and abuse.

9) Hunted any advanced philosophy such as the one developed by Hermes Trismegistus. All schools that taught his knowledge were reduced to ashes.

10) With the help of the Spanish Empire, tortured and sacrificed the Aztec and Inca people. Tens-of-millions were exterminated.

The Church's actions have repeatedly proven that it is first a political mechanism before a true religious institution. However, they present themselves as an instrument of God before an instrument of self-interest. Even the *New Testament* is secondary to their political will. They've demonstrated that by institutionalizing doctrine that isn't *New Testament*. It would appear that they're more so concerned with control and not the enlightenment of their followers. For example, the Church:

1) Created dogma like Purgatory,[31] Indulgences, and Auricular Confessions,[32] and purposely tricked the human spirit.

a. The idea of Purgatory was created as an instrument of fear and control, and it was actually first introduced by two Greek inventors in the second century, Clement of Alexandria and Origen.[33] Afterward, it evolved into its present form.

b. To compliment the idea of Purgatory and to reinforce their power, the leaders of the Church also created another tool of control called Indulgences. Indulgences were pieces of paper with Latin writing on them that reduced the amount of time a person would spend in Purgatory. Only an individual ordained by the Catholic Church was able to issue them. They normally issued them for a price.

c. And the Confessional was designed as an apparatus for the guilty to turn him or herself in. Moreover, it was a mechanism to reinforce the Church's position as God's sole representative, and as a device for the priests to exercise authority and control over the common people. In his book, *The History of the Confessional*, John Henry Hopkins states, *"it is in the Confessional that the priesthood wields their vast and secret power over the people. It is by the Confessional that they rivet the chains of superstition upon the conscience and the soul.[34]*

2) Portrayed an image of Jesus as a common man with a common weakness by convincing their members that Jesus drank wine. The holy ones like Jesus didn't need or desire a material substance to alter their state of mind.

Wine was given to the flock by the Church to get them "high" and to keep them easily susceptible, not for their benefit, and let's not forget that intoxicated people are looser with their wallets. I guess someone forgot *Ephesians 5:18*, and *Luke 1:15*: *"Do not get drunk on wine, which leads to debauchery. Instead, be filled with the Spirit."*-- (Ephesians 5:18) *"For he will be great in the sight of the Lord. He is never to take wine or other fermented drink, and he will be filled with the Holy Spirit even before he is born."*--(Luke 1:15)

3) Fixated the Catholic consciousness more on the vessel than the spark that was within, and the Catholic Church seems to give more importance to Jesus' mother, Mary, than Jesus.

By pushing ideas that focus the consciousness away from the Christ Consciousness, an individual doesn't receive the same blessings as they would by focusing on the Christ Consciousness. It would appear that the Catholic institution accidentally or purposely disempowered the potential of the Catholic people. Don't get me wrong, Mary was amazing and she carried Jesus. It's important to remember the vessel but not more so than "The Light" that was within.

It's also fair to mention that the Virgin Mary wasn't the only virgin mother. Krishna and others are acclaimed as sons of virgins.[35]

4) Created a vast administrative infrastructure (cardinals, archbishops, archdeacons, priests, monks, nuns, etc.) which is unscriptural. *"The Church, in the sense of the clergy, is not to be found in the whole Bible."*[36] It can be said that they created their grand institution to present themselves as the only gateway to The Eternal and to legitimize their existence. In keeping with this idea, for centuries they presented themselves as the only entity authorized to interpret the *Scriptures*. That wrongly led to a monopoly over the holy literature, which in turn wrongly strengthened their position as the only entity capable of interpreting the *Bible* and communing with The Formless Lord.

It would seem that the simplicity of Jesus' Church was lost to Roman secularism, ambition, and politics. Jesus never envisioned such a grand infrastructure and hierarchy, as presented by the Holy-Roman Catholic Church, to mediate the affairs of God. However, a massive infrastructure does help control the ruled and consolidate the power of the rulers.

5) And convinced the Catholics that God appoints the Pope and the Pope is The Great Architect's earthly representative. However, the belief isn't scriptural and the *Bible* actually speaks against an earthly head. *"But do not be called Rabbi; for One is your Teacher, and you are all brothers. Do not call anyone on earth your father; for One is your Father, He who is in heaven."*--(Matthew 23:8-9).

There was a time when the appointment of a Pope was actually approved by the Roman Emperor.[37] The Pope is as ordained as King James or Caligula were, and they all proclaimed a divine right so to maintain and enhance their power, wealth, and control The same applies to the Papacy. The people are taught to think of the Pope as appointed by God so to limit any resistance to the Catholic Church's authority.

The Catholic Church and the Pope expect complete submission and obedience from their followers, even when they've behaved in corrupt, scandalous, immoral, and fallible ways.[38] Under the leadership of the Popes, the world within their grasp went through centuries of darkness. From the 4th to the 15th century, the Church dominated the nations that were under her influence, and in that time period, civilizations regressed. It was a period of feeble-mindedness known as the age of darkness. The damage done during that time is still with the Christian world. Kingdoms like the Ottoman Empire didn't do much better, and the advancements they did demonstrate were not native developments but mostly inventions they took from the people they invaded. Of which, substantial knowledge was dismissed because it wasn't permitted by their governing ideology.

The Catholic Church is the largest and wealthiest religion in the world, but unfortunately, they've behaved as most other empires have. They manipulated the beliefs of those they could so to expand and maintain their power, wealth, and control. The supposed truths communicated by the Church might not be so truthful.

I'm not certain when the Church first decided to stage-manage their followers, but if I were to make a guess, I would suggest that it was soon after the Roman Empire took an interest in the establishment.

Sometime in the 300s, the Roman Empire took control of what is now the Catholic Church. After which is when the Church created the *New Testament* and began murdering other Christians and destroying other Christian *Gospels*. They were attempting to consolidate their influence. Like drug-dealers who murder the competition to expand their market share.

It should be remembered that the Roman Empire, before the conversion to Christendom, worked to eliminate every Christian from the Roman dominion because the Christians were not so easily ruled by Roman values. The Roman values questioned by the House of Jesus were those that condoned the exploitation, slavery, murder, and thievery of others. Fortunately, the Roman Empire was unable to eliminate the Christians. Mystically, Christendom continued to multiple. With the killing of one Christian, two would rise to take his or her place. Persecuting the Christians only provoked the growth of the faith.

Unfortunately, the Romans employed another tactic when the first failed. They strategically infiltrated Christendom. Instead of attempting to wipe the Christians off the face of the earth, the Empire embraced them, became them, and took control of them from within. Burdening the Christians not only with a secular leadership, but also with the luggage the Empire brought with it. For example, the fight between the Catholics and the Muslims is a carry-over of the conflict between Rome and the Persian Empire. Islam conquered the territories of the Persian's and the Catholic Church inherited the property of Rome. The elites of those lands still held a grudge and continued the struggle but under a different banner.

It's difficult to deny that the Church was infiltrated by political ambitions and that happening led to corrupt and fallible behaviour. That happening is also responsible for the decline in the belief of God. Religion has deceived people one too many times and the mass exodus was the reaction to the lies. Regrettably, those who stepped outside the Church had few options to turn to. The Church dominates the religious market.

Nonetheless, don't be mistaken, their shady behaviour isn't an indication that there is no God, nor is it an indication that the Church facilitates zero truth. As in the case of Islam, the truths of the metaphysical are far more prevalent than the fabrications and the political injections. It's a matter of distinguishing between truths and falsehoods, and understanding religion as a political mechanism before a servant of God.

By addressing the politics played by, for example, the Church, a person only steps that much closer to The Formless. Concurrently, the arguments put forth to deny God are effectively neutralized. God is self-evident and there is no viable argument that denies God--individuals such as Richard Dawkins try but their arguments fall short. Likewise, the corruption of religion is self-evident, and the corruption of religion is what individuals such as Dawkins depend on to deny The Great Architect. Popular culture too highlights the corruption of religion to imply that there is no God. But their logic is flawed. There is a distinction between God and religion.

Acknowledging the corruption also gives rise to the opportunity to correct the divergence and to return to the humble and universal nature that is the Church of Jesus--before the corporate infrastructure, the countless administrators, the political injections, the divisions, and the selfish ambitions.

The Church acts more like a political and economic institution than an instrument of Jesus, but that isn't to say that the followers of the Church are politically motivated or selfish. The followers of the Church are good people with good intentions. The true Catholic, like the true Muslim and the true Hebrew, efforts to live a God oriented life, and as with all of them, there is a distinction between the institution and the people. With that in mind, this manuscript challenges religious institutions and not their members. The follower did what every person should do and he or she went looking for God. It isn't the members I question but the institutions. I question them when they take advantage of a person's innocence and willingness to follow.

After speaking with a few Catholic friends about such things as the crusades, the Spanish Inquisition, and the atrocities committed towards the First Nations, they were passively aware of the corruption within the Church and felt very much ashamed and helpless. They were able to draw the distinction between the politically motivated and the celestially inspired, but felt as if they were powerless to exorcize the Church of its political component. To the detriment of the God seeker, a mist surrounds the nature of the Church.

The corruptions of the Church are obvious, and the Church is an excellent example of a religion that unjustly presents itself as incorruptible, but can be proven opposite. Other religious institutions also have their share of dirt. They too house similar examples. They too were infiltrated. For that reason, it would be reasonable for a person to question the doctrine and the history written by people, groups, nations, or institutions that repeatedly acted corruptly. It would also be reasonable for a person to attempt to discover truths through other sources and then get back to their faith. It would be sensible to exercise the only real option available and rationally rebuild. A temporary separation of God and religion is required.

However, there is no need to question all information presented by religions. Examine the stuff that stimulates feelings of discomfort, divides people from people, pits one against another, condones violence, glorifies plunder, disregards the humanity of a people or person, challenges reasonable knowledge, restricts the unlimited power of The Formless, provokes a sense of fear to gain obedience, exemplifies an economic agenda, denies the truth in other religions, or promotes institutional mediation to connect with the heavens.

Although the corruptions and the deceptions of the "post-Roman" Catholic Church are used to make a general point about religious institutions, again, the Catholic Church does teach the truths pertaining to the celestial--just like every other religion does. They've also produced amazing holy saints such as St Francis, St George, and St Simeon Stylites. Not only that, because of the astronomical amount of wealth the Church possesses, the Church has the potential to be the greatest of virtuous institutions the world has ever seen. But first, they would have to apologize for the many devilish deeds carried out in the name of religion--a confession that seems unlikely. To admit that mistakes were made is to admit the Church is fallible and not divine. For what is divine is infallible and forever truthful. If a religious institution is repeatedly proven corrupt, the people will naturally question the remainder of the doctrine they've pushed. That would obviously threaten the power of the Church and their ability to motivate a people to behave in a specific way.

If I were to make a recommendation, it would not include walking away from the Catholic Church. That would only create more denominations. The reason they came about in the first place. Further disunity isn't the solution, and an examination of the Church is required. But seventeen-hundred years of political games echo the halls of the Vatican, where to begin to clean the contamination?

St Francis could talk to animals and calm beasts. He was also habitually subject to the stigmata, and he did what he could to keep the Church from straying.

St George is one of the most recognized Christian military saints and one of the bravest martyrs of Christendom. As a soldier in Diocletian's army, in early 300 AD, George was instructed to renounce his faith and adopt the Pagan belief system. On his refusal, he was executed, but not before giving all his wealth to the poor.

St Simeon Stylites spent 40 days in a hut without any food or water. This is a common story found in other religions, and only those touched by The Eternal are able to perform such a feat. The human condition houses an organ that produces the nutrients a person needs to live, and the saints who are able to live without food and water for a prolonged period of time were granted access to that specific organ by The Eternal.

The British actively distorted cultural and historical truths to further their imperialistic agenda. It can be said that most of the empires that came and went also practiced the art of conditioning falsehoods.[39] Maybe, that's why the descendants of the Roman Empire, the Church, did it too. In the end, they all had the same goal in mind, to place themselves as supreme in the conquered cultures literature and thought. That was done to legitimize and strengthen their hold over the general public and the generations to come. Generations bred ignorant to the truth can't challenge and only God knows the true extent of the deception. Likewise, most people are born into religion and haven't truly endeavoured to discover what The Formless is, and innocently, some believe in the political spin that's presented as God sent.

"Jesus said, 'The Pharisees and the scribes have taken the keys of Knowledge and hidden them. They themselves have not entered, nor have they allowed to enter those who wish to. You, however, be as wise as serpents and as innocent as doves.'"--(Gospel of Thomas)

Religion was infiltrated and employed by the elite ruling class to take a flock's wealth, to motivate a people to war and to plunder, to alienate the general public from ideas and knowledge that might bring them to a better understanding of God, to propagate fear, to control the herd, and to reinforce their status as the upper class. The footprints left by the infiltration are more than evident. Religions were corrupted. However, that isn't to suggest that God is. Friend, there is a distinction.

Prophets and Politics

Unless touched by The Eternal, it's impossible to touch The Eternal. But touch those who The Formless touched and the path to The Great Architect will reveal itself. The essences of Jesus, Buddha, Nanak, Zarathushtra, Mohammad, etc. were one with The Lord. All are guides to the path. Pick any of them to lead, and through your mind's eye, attempt to touch.

However, some religions claim that their prophet is the only gateway to The Formless. For example, the Christians claim that Jesus is the shepherd, and Islam claims that Mohammad is the divine guide. Furthermore, they claim that all others are false. But, each of the holy from the many religions performed miracles, each revealed The Eternal, and countless people have utilized the spirit of each as a gateway to The Absolute. Accordingly, any of the holy can provide reception to The Celestial.

So, why are the holy on opposite ends?

After moving aside generations of political spin and digging through centuries of religious riddles, most religious institutions claim their prophet is the only for several reasons:

1) To empower the elite and their agenda.
2) To reinforce the religious institution's reputation as the only holder of divine truth.
3) To instil a sense of superiority within the followers.
4) And to motivate people to war and conquer. . (To learn more about the strategies occasionally used to convince people to war, please read *War 101*).

It's much easier to convince a people to war against other people when they believe that the other represents a false prophet. It's much easier to convince a people to war if they feel that they're freeing another people from their false prophet. And it's much easier to convince a people to war if they feel that The Formless guides only them.

Some religions proclaim that their prophet is the only gateway to The Absolute, and it's my belief that politics played centuries ago, today, prevent those religions from acknowledging the others. But regardless of what those religious institutions may believe, regardless of the centuries that divide the baker and the cake, any and all of the prophets can provide a gateway. That is, so long as an individual's faith in The Absolute is true and steadfast.

A Rose is Still a Rose

Some believe that Jesus is God and all those who do not give God that name will burn in hell. I must ask--what about the billions who existed before the birth of Jesus, they never had an opportunity to know the name, did they all, by default, fall to hell?

I guess if God was cruel, that might be true.

The same people who believe the above also suggest, regardless of a person's character, that by simply accepting the name "Jesus", an individual will automatically enter heaven after death. However, that isn't what the *New Testament* advocates. If only the entrance to heaven was that easy to pass through. The passage below proposes that a corrupt character is too big to fit through the gateway to heaven--no matter if he accepted the name of Jesus.

> *"For it is easier for a camel to go through a needle's eye, than for a rich man to enter into the kingdom of God."*-- (Luke 18:25)

It isn't the name a person gives The One Divine or the image a person chooses to see The One in, it's a person's state of consciousness that determines existence after death, life on earth, and love for The One. Besides, a rose is still a rose no matter the name it's given.

If a person wishes to name The Eternal Energy, Jesus, well, that's all good. But the fact of the matter is that if another chooses to call that same Eternal Energy another name such as Allah, Ahura Mazda, Govind, Jehovah, or Waheguru, that too is all good. They're all attempting to describe The One.

Again, it's not the name but an individual's state of consciousness that determines their life, their death, and their love for The One. It's the only thing that truly makes universal sense.

If No Jesus

If no Abraham,
if no Moses,
if no Jesus,
if no Mohammad,
if no Nanak,
would there be the One?

If no Gospels,
if no Qur'an,
if no Gathas,
if no Granth,
would there be God?

Why do we allow for the divisions when in the beginning and the end, there is only One? We reinforce the divisions because each believes that they're the only with the truth. Each believes that their prophet or their book is the absolute.

But most prophets and most holy books have much in common. Each taught and teaches the person to live through the better half of the mind's duality and to live a God conscious life.

Just as there are commonalities, there are also differences, and people believe in either reincarnation, the Garden, or the Day of Judgement. Disconnected from all the arguments, all the arguments are valid. Conversely, there is an absolute just as there is for everything scientifically known about the Universe. I don't know what that absolute is, and when you sit down and give it thought, it doesn't really matter. The commonalities prescribe one mean and all ends are reached by travelling the same road and stepping on the same stone--all ends are reached by developing the beautiful half of the mind and the soul. The beautiful half of the mind gives live to such happenings as humility, compassion, love, a desire for truth, and so on. Whatever the fixed is, each who travels that road and steps on that stone is subject to the absolute, regardless of whether they were aware or unaware of that truth.

So, let it be reincarnation, the Garden, or the Day of Judgement. It doesn't matter. The true Christian, the true Sikh, the true Hebrew, and the true Muslim all hold hands, travel the same road, and step on the same stone.

Stepping Stone

Judgement Day, Liberation, or the perfect secular existence, all require the same from the faithful. A heavenly incarnation, a righteous resurrection, or a return to the Garden, all ends are reached by guiding the growth of the consciousness and the soul. Regardless of what you believe, all ends are reached by conquering the parts of the mind that block the divine and corrupt the human potential--all ends are reached by allowing the beautiful mind to hold the soul of an angel.

The two foremost variables, the soul of an angel and the beautiful (the better half of the mind, where live love, compassion, truth, humility, self-restraint, virtue, kindness, etc.), with them as your comrades, the outcome after death is most favourable. No matter if a person believes in some sort of individual judgement after the body falls, or if they believe that all will rise together and stand before The Court of the Lord.

So, stand on opposite ends but respect the outlook of the other. Please appreciate that the journey is one and we all step on the same stone.

Enemies

A common enemy has united nations. A common enemy can unite the world. Do not look to another to see an enemy, look to the ways of the world.

Poverty--Hunger--Illiteracy. Consumption--Waste--Pollution. Jealousy--Hate--Divisions. Greed--War--Oppression.

"A new command I give you: Love one another. As I have loved you, so you must love one another. By this everyone will know that you are my disciples, if you love one another."--(John 13:34-35)

Caught

When a moral crime is committed,
there is no escaping prison.
Caught by many, many method;
there is no outrunning consequence.
In the brain if not by body pain.
By Godly laws if not by cage.
Man's hand or The Divine's Hand,
subject is every soul that strays.

"If you do a thing openly or do it in secret, then surely Allah is Cognizant of all things."--(Qur'an 33:54)

Hell and Stuff

Some religious ideas, upon examination, appear man inspired. Ideas like "the Rapture". "The Rapture" is an idea created by a common man[40] and *"it is a fact that no Christian churches, congregations or fellowships that existed prior to 1830 proclaimed a 'rapture' doctrine."*[41] The idea of "the Rapture" was created by John Darby of the Plymouth Brethren movement.[42]

If you're wondering what "the Rapture" is, according to the proponents of the theory, supposedly, there will come a day when only those who believe in Christ will receive salvation. In that moment, and within a flash, they'll be transported to heaven. The people remaining on the planet will endure some sort of trial and punishment.

Not surprisingly, ever since the invention of the idea, every generation who believed in "the Rapture" thought the phenomenon would happen in their lifetime.

"The Rapture" doesn't seem to be the only idea inspired by man. After inspection, ideas such as hell and the Devil also appear as constructs.[43]

It's very plausible that the Egyptian belief in the Underworld inspired the idea of hell. After which, the Hebrews borrowed the idea, fine-tuned it, and then transmitted it to the religions that followed. The Christians and the Muslims both stem from the Jewish tradition.

Interestingly, the belief in the underworld is an adaptation of the idea presented in the *Tablets of Thoth*. In which, the underworld is a place of light. The *Tablets of Thoth* are a better account of the Egyptian belief system than the nonsense mainstream archaeology has presented. Archaeologists prefer to depict the ancient Egyptians as superstitious and intellectually inferior people, but after a closer examination, they were far from ignorant.

However, through errors in transmission or intentional manipulation, the Jewish idea of hell is a place of darkness and ruled by the Devil. That said, none of the ancient Jewish literature reflects the popular idea of hell.[44]

The creation of the notion of hell was inspired by a desire to keep the masses scared, submissive, and obedient to the elite. In fear, people will do almost anything to relinquish that fear. The Greeks used similar devices. Thomas Thayer, in his book, *The Origins and History of the Doctrine of Endless*, writes:

> *"Any one at all familiar with the writings of the ancient Greeks or Romans, cannot fail to note how often it is admitted by them that the national religions were the inventions of the legislator and the priest, for the purpose of governing and restraining the common people...The object of this sacred fraud was to impress the minds of the multitude with religious awe, and command a more ready obedience of their part.... Of Course, in order to secure obedience, they were obliged to invent divine punishments for the disobedience of what they asserted to be divine law.*"[45]

Unfortunately, the idea of hell has existed for so long that it's an idea taken as absolute and above debate--not to mention that every person is born with the abilities of a sinner and a saint. Why would God forever condemn what God knowingly made? Unless of course, God is truly cruel and created us only to see us burn and bleed, an idea that several religions facilitate.[46]

I do not deny the negative metaphysical consequences that spring from sinful motion. Nor do I deny heaven. I only challenge the popular notion of hell--a depiction that illustrates eternal damnation, eternal suffering, and eternal torture. It doesn't make sense for God to give the ability to sin and then forever condemn the human being for it.

The foremost consequence of sin is that it contaminates the aura a person emanates, and a polluted aura creates distance between the person and God's Spirit. God's Spirit is what liberates the person.

The popular idea of hell doesn't make sense. Neither does this idea of a cosmic battle between good and evil. Nor this creature called the Devil. The idea of a personified entity capable of challenging the power of God is a fictional account.

In view of the fact that God is the creator of all, why would God create an enemy or entity capable of equalling, challenging, and overthrowing? The idea of a cosmic battle and the idea of the Devil were ideas created to scare the people into obedience, to explain elements of nature not understood like the destructive power of the Universe, and to compliment and reinforce the false notion of hell. And "no", I don't think the Devil has the potential to overthrow The Creator of all. Everything is under the control of The Lord and Master. Moreover, The Great Architect dwells in all realms. If there is a hell, then God is the master there too.

The popular idea of the Devil tells a story of an entity who was once in the light of God, the perfect existence. But because of his jealousy of humanity, he rejected God and eventually left the light to destroy humanity. Two questions for those who believe--Is it possible for a negative like jealousy to exist in the light of God, and is God so weak that he can't prevent the Devil from interfering in human affairs? Jesus once said, as recorded in the *Gospel of Thomas*, *"Whoever believes that the All itself is deficient is (himself) completely deficient."*

Interestingly, the popular idea of the Devil doesn't seem to have a foundation within the *New Testament*.[47] Even in the *Old Testament*, Satan isn't made out to be as powerful as Satan is popularly known as.

Again, I do not deny the existence of the negative/destructive energy or the positive/creative energy within the Universe. However, the ideas of good and evil seem manmade and the phenomena those ideas attempt to describe were intentionally created by The Eternal.

In a sense, you can call the negative energy the Devil, however, without a sovereign will and similar to the idea of gravity, a Principle of the Universe. A Principle of the Universe created by The One Lord Master and under the authority of The One Lord Master.

The idea of burying the dead, so the corpse can be resurrected and collectively judged, is another concept rooted in popular misconception. This notion also limits the power of The Formless and confuses the mind's eye. The idea is confusing because it implies that God needs a blueprint to reconstitute the human condition. That interpretation suggests that God isn't as almighty as God truly is.

God doesn't need a bag of bones to create when with breath God created everything known and unknown. And if the body were meant to live forever, the design of the body would allow the body to live forever. That is the way of the Universe--that is the way of The Eternal.

The ways of The Eternal are not as mysterious as religions have presented them as. That is, after a person gains a firm understanding; an understanding buried underneath religious riddles and political spin that constantly misdirect the God seeker. As such, the person has little choice but to question before accepting a truth.

In some cases, the messages of the holy were changed. In other cases, religions misinterpreted the messages of the saintly or inserted their own selfish beliefs, and the misinterpreted and/or inserted values have existed for so long that they've had time to mix with the facts, and along the way, they've managed to recruit passionate mullahs, clergymen, preachers, and priestesses.

Sin and Forgiveness

Several pages back, I mentioned the idea of the Catholic Confessional. The idea of the Confessional touches a very important concept. One common to most popular religions and an idea taught by the truly holy like Jesus--to daily request forgiveness for one's sins.

The fact of the matter is that we all sin for one reason or another, and we all house the cognitive agents that allow the person to sin. But what is a sin? Both the biblical and the historical usages deduced conclude that a sin is to prevent a person or the self from using or developing the better half of the mind's condition, and to ignore the divinity within the self or within others. The beautiful half of the mind's duality is the portion of the mind that houses the phenomena of compassion, humility, truth, and virtue.

Although the Confessional touches on a very important idea, I do not agree with their notion that an earthly intermediary is required to ask God for forgiveness. An individual can develop a personal relationship with The Eternal. Through focus of consciousness, an individual can directly ask The Lord to show pity and to forgive a person for their mistakes. Only then is an individual free of their sins.

All the holy individuals I've had the opportunity to learn from stressed the fact that there are temporary consequences after the body perishes. Fortunately, God isn't cruel and although the person is born with the programming to sin, God also created a universal law so to save the individual from the consequences of those discretions. With focus of consciousness, humbly ask The Fathomless to show pity and to forgive.

Even though The Eternal gave the person the ability to sin and prescribed consequences for it, The Formless also gave the human condition a remedy. The Eternal isn't cruel but loving.

Forgiving others is something to value as well, and it's as important as asking for forgiveness for the self.

"For if you forgive others their trespasses, your heavenly Father will also forgive you, but if you do not forgive others their trespasses, neither will your Father forgive your trespasses."--(Matthew 6:14-15)

The Doctrine Within

Sometimes it's arduous determining what's what, especially when there's a preacher, pastor, mullah, brahmin, or minister countering all reasonable questions with the phrase, "just have faith". However, a person like me has faith and a person like me loves The Formless. But a person like me can't ignore the crooked politics played and the manner in which elements of some doctrine challenge the soul. Inspire they do feelings of confusion and discomfort.

I guess, at times, I'm a little too headstrong to allow the rhetoric to shut down my mind and the Inner Light. I can't accept everything presented as God sent. And from the looks of it, it appears that I'm not the only one. From the looks of it, I'm not the only one who can't ignore the spiritual, biological, and cognitive reactions.

I've spoken with many who also experience the same. They too feel as if something inside of them activates when they attempt to comprehend elements of some doctrine, like a house alarm after a parameter breach. I've spoken with many who've also experienced the same. They too felt as if something inside of them was intrinsically privy to the true nature of The Supreme Light, and when that nature is under question or information opposite to that intrinsic information is absorbed by the mind, that something activates feelings of confusion and discomfort--to alert the person of potential danger.

The inner alarm is what makes it arduous, and the inner alarm is what sways a person like me to question the preachers, pastors, mullahs, brahmins, and ministers. Their logic sometimes sounds like spin, the type propagated by G.W. Bush when he was trying to convince the Americans that Iraq possessed weapons of mass destruction. And when I hear them counter my reasonable questions with phrases like, "just have faith", it feels as if they're working to convince me that one plus one equals four.

Every individual is born with this intrinsic alarm, and it's designed to assist the person in his or her search for God knowledge. However, it can be hidden, just as Mencius believed that the good in a person can be disguised. In this case, inaccurately constructed God knowledge can bury the intrinsic alarm. If that happens, an individual's value system is ripe to justify happenings such as the crusades, the conversion of non-Muslims, the repression of the Indigenous, the murder of the Cathars, bloodshed in Jerusalem, and a man-induced Armageddon.

Advantageously, just as the good in a person can be again, as Mencius suggested, with the appropriate nourishment, how can the buds and sprouts of the intrinsic not again appear?

Sometimes it's arduous determining what's what, especially when there's a preacher, pastor, mullah, brahmin, or minister countering all reasonable questions with the phrase, "just have faith". However, a person like me has faith and a person like me loves The Formless. But a person like me can't ignore the crooked politics played and the manner in which elements of some doctrine challenge the soul. Inspire they do feelings of confusion and discomfort.

God is Within

The Eternal Commander and Chief created all, and in doing so, The Eternal infused the essence that is God within everything that exists. Without that essence, there would be nothing to support the Universe and all its principles and inhabitants, including the human condition's breath of life. For that reason, every single human being is equal to another.

This idea of God within the individual troubles one of the most popular religions, and I think it's because they don't fully understand the idea. It seems as if the belief of God within the human condition implies to Christendom that the person is God. However, that isn't the case. God is within all creation and separate from (onto thyself). But without the essence of The Primal Void, nothing can exist.

Not surprisingly, the above notion wasn't foreign to the Christian's before Constantine created the *New Testament,* especially among the Gnostics. But Constantine didn't like the idea. Such ideas would discourage the Christian from invading other people's places, taking their possessions, murdering them, and stealing their land to expand the Roman Empire. To hurt another is to hurt the God within them, and why would anyone who appreciates the idea endeavour to hurt another knowing The Primal Void also feels it?

> *"Jesus said, 'If they say to you -where did you come from? Say to them--we came from the light, the place where the light came into being on its own accord and established [itself] and became manifest through their image. If they say to you--is it you? Say--we are its children, we are the elect of the Living Father. If they ask you--what is the sign of your father in you? Say to them--it is movement and repose.'"*--(Gospel of Thomas)

Countless saints have spoken of God in such a manner. Great philosophers such as Hermes Trismegistus and Aristotle too expressed the idea. The All-Mind is within all minds.

They also articulated that to discover The Light within (God's essence) is one of the highest life purposes. But be warned, the task is extremely difficult and mastery of meditation, of internal vibrations, and of the mind are a prerequisite. The end goal is to allow the identical self to consume the self.

The purpose is to allow The Light (God) within to govern the mind and body so to eventually merge with The Supreme Light. When The Light within is discovered, nurtured, and finally merged with The Supreme Light, an individual is considered one with The Primal Void and The Primal Void is considered one with the individual. It's been said by countless saints, when an individual does reach that state of being, there is little difference between the two.

When an individual does achieve such a state of being, they are no longer subject to the principles of the Universe that govern life and death. The potential for immortality is the individual's but not immortality of the physical. Death can be overcome.

So, search for The Light within, God is closer to you than some popular religions have propagated. As Jesus expressed, the true church is within the body fortress.

God is within and there's a concentration of the God essence within the heart and the heart chakra. The Egyptians believed so strongly in the idea that when they would mummify a dead body, they would throw away the brain and pay overwhelming attention to the heart. The heart had more value than the brain.

The Egyptians were not and are not the only people who give the heart and the heart chakra importance. Most other spiritual paths that utilize the chakras of the human condition also accommodate the same understanding.

> *"Wherever I look, I see that One Lord alone. Deep within each and every heart, He Himself is contained. ||1||Pause||"*--(Sri Guru Granth Sahib Ji, ang 387 of 1430)

The person is a body fortress and within is The Great Architect. Not only that, the human body is constituted by divine instruments such as the Ida and Pingali, and these tools are capable of connecting the person with God.

The Eternal Commander and Chief created all, and in doing so, The Eternal infused the essence that is God within everything that exists. Without that essence, there would be nothing to support the Universe and all its principles and inhabitants.

Jesus never wrote the *Gospels*. Nor did Mohammad write the *Qur'an*. For that reason, the arrangement of words, sentences, and paragraphs in the *Bible* and the *Qur'an* are open to interpretation.

If Jesus had written the *Gospels*, if Mohammad had written the *Qur'an*, and if they were perfectly transmitted generation to generation, there would be no confusion, no denomination, and no twisting of the text.

God's Words

The most outspoken religious institutions--Christianity, Judaism, and Islam--repeatedly claim that their Holy Texts contain the only Words and Ideas of God. Absolute and incorrupt. Each also claims that their doctrine is the only path to The Formless.

However, in the case of the *New Testament*, Jesus never wrote what he thought or preached and words were attributed to him decades after he ascended into "The White Light". Men other then he wrote the *Gospels* and each writer plausibly mixed in his own personality. Clear evidence of that are the disagreements and the contradictions between the different versions of the *Bible*, such as those between the Latin Vulgate and the King James Version. And clear confirmation of that are the inconsistencies between the authors of the *Gospels*.

> *"Mark says that Jesus was crucified the day after the Passover meal was eaten (Mark 14:12; 15:25) and John says he died the day before it was eaten (John 19:14)... Luke indicates in his account of Jesus's birth that Joseph and Mary returned to Nazareth just over a month after they had come to Bethlehem and performed the rites of purification (Luke 2:39), whereas Mathew indicates they instead fled to Egypt (Matt. 2:19-22)."* [48]

Even though names are given, there is no way to confirm who actually wrote the *New Testament*, [49] and author Jack Nelson-Pallmeyer, in his book, *Is Religion Killing Us?: Violence in the Bible and the Quran* (2005), makes an interesting observation about one of the supposed, Mathew.

> *"Matthew is often an unreliable witness of Jesus. In his parables Jesus repeatedly exposes key actors in the oppressive system, only to have Matthew present those exposed as 'God figures' that Matthew blesses with the*

authority of Jesus' voice. These 'God figures' consistently send people to the torturers or to other terrible punishments."

In all fairness, it's very possible that the authors of the *Gospels* were guided by a Divine Will, and thus making their words the Words of God. But the originals are lost and over the centuries words where changed, translated, dropped, or added. What we have today is not what originally was and maybe that's why there are contradictions. Author John Vaughan asserts:

> *"...the original writers were preserved from all error by the direct assistance of the Holy Ghost, this Divine assistance does not extend to the individual monks or friars, or other scribes, however holy, who sat down, pen in hand, to reproduce the original text."[50]*

Furthermore, the *Gospels* were initially communicated orally[51] and when the practice of recording them in writing came to be, unintentional and intentional mistakes were made.

> *"...scribes occasionally altered the words of their sacred texts to make them more patently orthodox."[52]*

> *"At times scribes would make intentional changes as they copied. For example, they would correct what they believed to be a spelling error in their source text. And even the best of scribes also sometimes made unintended errors."[53]*

> *"There were thousands and thousands of copyists busily employed in the monasteries and scriptoriums through the world. Through want of observation or through carelessness or weariness, or on account of difficult or partially effaced writing, how easy it was to mistake a letter, or to omit a word or a particle; yet such an omission is*

capable of altogether changing the sense of an entire passage. The accidental dropping of even a single letter may sometimes make a striking difference. "[54]

"Attestations of variants within the lectionary tradition are so manifold that there is little plausibility in the theory that at the beginning of the lectionary tradition there was one specific text set up for liturgical reading that was then copied as a unity and in the course of its history increasingly brought into agreement with the mainstream. It appears to be more likely that different text forms fed into the lectionary tradition and were carefully copied and 'commonly and officially used.' "[55]

In relation, the contemporary English *Gospels* are all translations of translations of translations,[56] and the original *Gospels* didn't survive. What we have are translations of copies of the originals and not translations of the originals (autographs).[57] Bart Ehrman, an expert on the topic, writes:

"So rather than actually having the inspired words of the autographs (i.e., the originals) of the Bible, what we have are the error-ridden copies of the autographs." [58]

"We have only error-ridden copies, and the vast majority of these are centuries removed from the originals and different from them, evidently, in thousands of ways." [59]

"What good does it do to say that the words are inspired by God if most people have absolutely no access to these words, but only to more or less clumsy renderings of these words into a language, such as English, that has nothing to do with the original words?" [60]

Three centuries after the death of Jesus, under the guidance of Emperor Constantine (a politician), the Christian doctrine was solidified. But during the process, not all of the *Gospels* were included and knowledge was purposely hidden.[61] And debated doctrine such as--was Jesus God, the Son of God, or a mortal man--were arbitrarily put to rest by one person who was allegedly considered a heretic by the Christians,[62] and who's been repeatedly proven inaccurate by contemporary historians, Eusebius, the Emperor's religious advisor.[63] It's a fact that before Constantine consolidated the Christian doctrine, *"thousands of documents existed chronicling His life (Jesus' life) as a mortal man."*[64]

So, why would an emperor want to ally himself with God, or the Son of God, and not a mortal man? The answer is simple. God and the Son are more powerful than any man is. It's always more advantageous to ally with the more powerful.

Not only was the above doctrine challenged, many Christians also questioned dogma like that presented in *Apocalypse* (*Book of Revelation*). They considered it sacrilegious.[65]

Now, why would Constantine want such literature as part of the Christian doctrine? Divine punishment is required to keep the people obedient and dependent on the institution providing the means to salvation from that divine punishment. *Apocalypse* provides very descriptive images of that divine punishment. Those images create vivid pictures within the mind. That experience reinforces the overall idea of a divine punishment. Also, as every good emperor knows, the people must be willing to act violently to maintain and expand an empire. The violence within *Apocalypse* desensitizes a people to violence and contributes to that end.

It should be noted that before Constantine, the Christians were persecuted by the Roman Empire and their sacred books were destroyed. Not all of the recorded truths of Jesus and Christianity were available when Constantine decided to consolidate the Christian faith.[66]

During the melding process, there were Christians who didn't agree with Constantine's version of Christianity. However, they didn't object because they feared that the Emperor would punish them. Two actually did disagree and they were exiled.[67]

After Constantine's interference, what is now the Catholic Church remained and all other types of Christianity were persecuted,[68] and all competing *Gospels* were destroyed.[69] Any person or group opposed to the doctrine and *Bible* presented by the Church where depicted as an evil and then eliminated.

Before Constantine, the different Christian perspectives debated but they rarely resorted to violence. Even though some people propagated horrid opinions.[70]

> *"Blessed are the peacemakers, for they shall be called sons of God."*--(Matthew 5:9)

But after Constantine, violence was used to consolidate the *New Testament* and the power of those who held it. Something I think Jesus would probably disagree with. He believed in peace and not violence as the instrument best equipped to reveal God's Kingdom.

The unification of Christianity also included the conversion of the Catholic clergy into employees of Rome.[71] Afterward, they took the titles of the Roman Government and changed in demeanour to reflect their Roman status.[72] As you can guess, after the Romans gave importance to the Church, the Church began attracting power and wealth. Subsequently, *"power-hungry, greedy politicians began to take over positions of leadership".*[73]

Author David L. Dungan astutely recaps Constantine's interference in his book, *Constantine's Bible: politics and the making of the New Testament* (Fortress Press: Philadelphia, 2006).

"...the newly Christian emperor's efforts to influence virtually every aspect of his newfound ally, Catholic Christianity--from building new churches to paying clergy out of the state treasury, to intervening in church disputes, to convening councils of bishops and issuing edicts and making their decisions the law of the realm, to helping to determine the date for celebrating Easter to mandating Sunday as the universal day of worship, to outlawing heresy, to de facto implementations of Eusebius's 'acknowledged books' as the standard Bible of the Catholic Church."--(Page 94-95)

Although the Church suggests that the *Bible* is constituted by the only Words of God, the *Bible* doesn't make that assertion.[74] The Church, like the other popular religions, teaches that idea so to squash a person's logic, to limit any resistance, to pit one against another, to hide truth, to empire-build, and to disguise their political agenda and spin.

Regardless, the *Gospels* are still valuable and they're precious in the sense that they communicate important lessons and messages. They teach a person to live a moral, virtuous, and God orientated lifestyle. I was born and raised amongst the Christians and the true Christian is a person of excellent character. But to say that the *New Testament* is the only book with uncorrupted truth and the only that contains the Words of The Formless is inaccurate.

Judaism

Judaism also believes that their Texts are the only path to the truth and the only Words of God. However, Judaism suffers from the same problem Christianity does.

"The original text of Moses, and the ancient prophets, was destroyed with the temple and city of Jerusalem, by the Assyrians under Nebuchadnezzar; and the authentic copies

which replaced them, perished in the persecution of Antiochus. "[75]

"There is no original manuscript of the Bible extant anywhere throughout the world. All that we now possess are copies. Though the Old Testament writings were written three thousand years and more ago, we have no existing manuscript of the Hebrew Old Testament earlier than the ninth or tenth century after Christ. "[76]

"Believers like to think of 'sacred' texts as God's words, or at least as words inspired by God, but elite priestly writers were often guided by self-interest. They reinforced their own power by writing their privileges into the 'sacred' text." As Richard Horsley argues, the "'Priestly writers' of early postexilic times (when the Hebrew Scriptures were compiled and edited) reconstructed and virtually established a religious tradition as a way of legitimating the 'restored' Jewish social-political order. "[77]

Moreover, pieces of the *Old Testament* justify violence and immorality in the pursuit of a nation. I guess it's easier to convince people to kill other people and to take what they have, if God said they should kill and take.

"God, according to the Hebrew Scriptures, is a determined and powerful land thief who steals from others in order to give to the chosen people 'To your (Abram's) descendants I give this land, from the river of Egypt to the great river, the river Euphrates, the land of the Kenites, the Kenizzites, the Kadmonites, the Hittites, the Perizzites, the Rephiam, the Amorites, the Canaanites, the Girgashites, and Jebusites' (Gen 15:18-21). God-ordained land thievery is accompanied by divinely sanctioned genocide. After taking

the land, 'You must utterly destroy them... show them no mercy' (Deut 7:2). "[78]

Richard Heber Newton, an author from the late 1800s, writes:

"Thus the extermination of the Canaanites, for which the Hebrews pleaded long after the Divine order, and for which they had substantial warrant in Destiny's determination to rid the land of these corrupting tribes and make room for the noble life Israel was to develop, has been the stock argument of kings and soldiers for their bloody trade. Thus poor human consciences have been sorely hurt and troubled as men have read, in stories such as those of Jael and Sisera and Jacob and Esau, of act, which their better nature instinctively condemned." [79]

It would also appear that elements of the Jewish doctrine are not original to the Jewish people, and elements were borrowed from other cultures-- that notion effectively transforms their claim of exclusivity into mush. For example:

1) The idea of the devil isn't original to Judaism and the idea was borrowed from the doctrine of Zoroaster.[80]

2) The same applies to the ideas of Armageddon, Angels, Demons, and the resurrection of the dead. Those notions were introduced by the Zoroastrians and are not original to the Jewish people. Nor to the Christians and the Muslims.[81] It's believed Zoroaster's ideas were merged with Jewish beliefs during the enslavement of the Jews in Babylon, over 2 500 years ago.

3) The Sumerian myth of Gilgamesh is the inspiration behind the Garden of Eden.[82] The Persians and the Greeks also had their versions of the Garden before the Jewish people did. The Persians called it Heden and the Greeks named it Hesperidos.

) The story of the great flood was recorded by the Sumerians, and everal others, before the Hebrews documented it.[83]

slam

slam also believes that their Text is the true Words of God and all others are inaccurate. But Islam suffers from the same problems udaism and Christianity do.

Prophet Mohammad never wrote what he thought or preached and the Qur'an was compiled near twenty years after he ascended into "The White Light". Initially, like the *Gospels*, the messages were communicated orally and *"then noted in fragmentary fashion on a number of material supports. When discrepancies in the recitations became highly apparent, they were collected together to form the Qur'an and published by the caliph Uthman."*[84] Consequently, all messages the caliph didn't approve were destroyed.[85]

Moreover, as Bart Ehrman points to in his book, *The Orthodox Corruption of Scripture: The effect of early Christological controversies on the text of the New Testament* (1997):

> *"The oldest passages that can be dated securely, however, are the inscriptions on the Dome of the Rock (called the Mosque of 'Umar) in Jerusalem, built in 691. These inscriptions are more in the Qur'anic style than they are Qur'anic, strictly speaking, since they do not coincide perfectly with the text we possess."*--(Page 71)

Now, I do not deny Mohammad or the idea that God sent a messenger to communicate with him. However, it's more than plausible that during the transmission of Mohammad's messages, by other people, to the caliph, information was forgotten, misquoted, or introduced. In addition, caliph Uthman was not Mohammad. It's possible that what he thought was an authentic message from Mohammad wasn't. Furthermore, it's possible he didn't have all of Mohammad's messages when he decided to compose the *Qur'an*.

I do not deny the *New Testament*, the *Old Testament*, or the *Qur'an*, and I have found God within all of them. But none of them hold a monopoly on the truth and none are absolute. For each to claim that they're the only religion with the absolute and uncorrupted truth doesn't relate to the evidence. And when a religion teaches their followers that only their Holy Text will provide salvation, they're attempting to create divisions amongst the people of the planet for political or economic reasons.

Jesus was very real, and if I could I would die for him. But that doesn't mean I would die for the *New Testament*. The *New Testament* is more so a product of the Roman Empire and what she transformed to become, the Holy Roman Catholic Church.

Although Godly ideas are present within the *New Testament*, as are the opposite, and I just can't give my Godly essence to that which isn't.

In that respect, I guess I was mistaken when I wrote that I wouldn't die for the *New Testament*. I would happily die for that which is God-oriented. To that extent, I would die for pieces of it.

I have no loyalty towards religion. I give all my loyalty to the truth, regardless of truth's origins. May the truth reside in the *Old*, the *New*, the *Qur'an*, the *Vedas*, or the *Granth*. May the truth reside in the poor, the meek, the ugly, or the mud. I am a servant of that which is forever. I am a servant of The One God and God's Principles.

Endnotes

1. Thomas S. Asbridge, <u>The First Crusade: A New History</u> (Oxford University Press: New York, 2004), p. 1-3. / H.E.J. Cowdrey. "Pope Urban II's Preaching of the First Crusade." <u>The Crusades; the essential readings</u>. Ed. by Thomas F. Madden. (Blackwell Publishing: Oxford, UK; Malden, Ma, 2002). / Jonathan Riley-Smith. "Crusading as an Act of Love." <u>The Crusades; the essential readings.</u> Ed. by Thomas F. Madden. (Blackwell Publishing: Oxford, UK; Malden, Ma, 2002).

2. John France, <u>The Crusaders and the Expansion of Catholic Christendom, 1000-1714</u> (New York: Routledge, 2005). / Jonathan Riley-Smith, <u>The Crusades: a history; second edition</u> (Yale University Press: New Haven, 2005).

3. "Indian Residential Schools Settlement Agreement: May 8th, 2006." Indian Residential Schools Settlement--Official Court Website. [http://www.residentialschoolsettlement.ca/Settlement.pdf], January, 2009. / Art Gallery of Windsor, <u>New World--old world: eurocentric perceptions of first nations people and the landscape</u> (Windsor: Art Gallery of Windsor, 1997). / Tim Giago, <u>Children Left Behind: dark legacy of Indian mission boarding schools </u>(Clear Light Pub.: Santa Fe, N.M., 2006).

4. Joseph Perez, <u>The Spanish Inquisition: a history</u> (Profile: London, 2004).

5. James M. Blaut, <u>The Colonizer's Model of the World: geographical diffusionism and Eurocentric history</u> (Guildford Press: New York, 1993).

6. Jack Nelson-Pallmeyer, <u>Is Religion Killing Us?: violence in the Bible and the Quran</u> (Continuum International Publishing Group: New York, 2005), p. 33.

7. Jerrold M. Post, <u>Leaders and their Followers in a Dangerous World: the psychology of political behaviour</u> (Cornell University Press: New York, 2004), p. 139.

8. Charles Selengut, <u>Sacred Fury: understanding religious violence</u> (Rowman Altamira: California, 2003), p. 226.

9. Robert Spencer, <u>The Politically Incorrect Guide to Islam and the Crusades</u> (Regnery Publishing: America, 2005), p. 54.

10. Ibid., p. 107--120.

11. Ann Graham Brock, <u>Mary Magdalene, The First Apostle: The Struggle for Authority</u> (Harvard University Press: Massachusetts, 2002). / Meere Lester, <u>The Everything Mary Magdalene Book: The life and legacy of Jesus's most misunderstood disciple</u> (Adams Media: Cincinnati, OH, 2006). / Jean Leloup, <u>Gospel of Mary Magdalene</u> (Inner tradition: Vermont, 2002).

12. Adrian Thatcher, <u>The Savage Text: the use and abuse of the Bible</u> (Wiley-Blackwell: Malden, MA, 2008), p. 39-49.

13. Eugen J. Weber, <u>Apocalypses: prophecies, cults and millennial beliefs through the ages</u> (Random House of Canada: Toronto, 1999).

14. Ibid.

15. Alexander George and Jerrold M. Post, <u>Leaders and their Followers in a Dangerous World: the psychology of political behaviour</u> (Cornell University Press: New York, 2004), p. 135-136.

16. Charles Selengut, <u>Sacred Fury: understanding religious violence</u> (Rowman Altamira: California, 2003), p. 101.

17. Alexander George and Jerrold M. Post, Leaders and their Followers in a Dangerous World: the psychology of political behaviour (Cornell University Press: New York, 2004), p. 141.

18. Gershom Gorenberg, The End of Days: fundamentalism and the struggle for the Temple Mount (Free Press: New York, 2000). / Adrian Thatcher, The Savage Text: the use and abuse of the Bible (Wiley-Blackwell: United Kingdom, 2008), p. 57 -63. / Victoria Clark, Allies for Armageddon: the rise of Christian Zionism (Yale University Press: New Haven; London, 2007).

19. Charles Selengut, Sacred Fury: understanding religious violence (Rowman Altamira: California, 2003), p. 103.

20. Adrian Thatcher, The Savage Text: the use and abuse of the Bible

21. Patrick Brantlinger, Rule of Darkness: British literature and imperialism, 1830-1914 (Cornell University Press: Ithaca, N.Y., 1988). / Homi Bhabha, The Location of Culture (Routledge: London; New York, 2004). / Robert Giddings, ed. Literature and Imperialism (Macmillan: Houndmills, 1991).

22. David Criswell, The Rise and Fall of the Holy Roman Empire: from Charlemagne to Napoleon (Publish America: Maryland, 2005). / Desmond O'Grady, Beyond the Empire: Rome and the church from Constantine to Charlemagne (Crossroad Publishing: New York, 2001). / Nino Lo Bello, The Vatican Empire (Trident Press: New York, 1969).

23. Richard Heber Newton, The Right and Wrong Uses of the Bible (John W. Lovell, 1883), p. 50. [http://www.google.com/books?id=bww-AAAAYAAJ&dq=The+Right+and+Wrong+Uses+of+the+Bible]

24. Ernan McMullin, ed. The Church and Galileo (University of Notre Dame Press: Indiana, 2005).

25. Kent C. Condie and Robert E. Sloan, Origin and Evolution of Earth: principles of historical geology (Prentice Hall: NJ, 1998).

26. Robert Spencer, Religion of Peace?: why Christianity is and Islam isn't (Regnery Publishing: Washington, 2007), p. 111.

27. David Daniels and Jack T. Chick, Did the Catholic Church Give use the Bible? (Chick Publications: California: 2005) p. 57-59.

28. Kersten Holger, Jesus Lived in India: his unknown life before and after the crucifixion (Penguin Books: India, 2001) / Nicolas B. Notovitch, The Unknown Life of Jesus Christ (Nababharat: Calcutta, 1981) / Levi H. Dowling, The Aquarian Gospel of Jesus the Christ (Biblio Publishing, 2009) p. 83-137.

29. P.A.H. Seymour, The Birth of Christ: Exploding the Myth (Virgin Publishing: London, 1999). / Michael R. Monlar, The Star of Bethlehem: The Legacy of the Magi (Rutgers University Press: NJ, 1999). / Stephen Vidano, Director, The Star of Bethlehem, 2007.

30. John Cornwell, Hitler's Pope: the secret history of Pius XII (Viking: New York, 1999). / Gordon Charles Zahn, German Catholics and Hitler's War: a study in social control (Sheed and Ward: New York, 1962).

31. Jacques LeGoff, The Birth of Purgatory (University of Chicago Press: Chicago, 1981). / Loraine Boettner, Roman Catholicism--Chapter Ten: Purgatory (P & R Publishing: NJ, 1989)

32. Loraine Boettner, Roman Catholicism--Chapter Nine: The Confessional (P & R Publishing: NJ, 1989)

33. Jacques LeGoff, The Birth of Purgatory (University of Chicago Press: Chicago, 1981) p. 52.

34. John Henry Hopkins, The History of the Confessional (Harper: London, 1850) p. 11
[http://books.google.ca/books?id=hMIHAAAAQAAJ&pg=PR6&dq=The+Confessional+and+false]

35. S. Acharya, Suns of God: Krishna, Buddha and Christ Unveiled (Adventures Unlimited Press: Illinois, 2004) p.205-206. / The Vishnu Purana. Trans. by Horace Hayman Wilson: 1840. / Larry Charles, Director, Religulous, 2008.

36. Unknown, The Bible and the People (1853), p. 60.
[http://www.google.com/books?id=tjMEAAAQAAJ&dq=The+Bible+and+the+People]

37. Joseph Priestly, An History of the Corruption of Christianity (University of Lausanne, 1782), p.80-283.
[http://www.google.com/books?id=y6AUAAAAQAAJ&printsec=frontcover&dq=An+History+of+the+Corruption+of+Christianity]

38. Garry Wills, Papal Sin: structures of deceit (Image Books/Doubleday: New York, 2001)./ Brandon Toropov, The Complete Idiot's Guide to the Popes and the Papacy (Alpha Books: America, 2001), p. 47-56.

39. Edward W. Said, Culture and Imperialism (Random House: New York, 1993)

40. Dave MacPherson, The Rapture Plot (South Carolina: Millennium III Publishers, 2000). / David B. Currie, Rapture: The end-times error that leaves the bible behind (Sophia Institute Press: Manchester, NH, 2004).

41. Wilson H. Speed, Rapture: A Dangerous Deception (Xulon Press: Longwood, Fl, 2009) p. 113.

42. Ibid., p. 115.

43. Alice K. Turner, The History of Hell (Harcourt Brace & Company: New York, 1993). / "What the hell is Hell?" Tentmaker Ministries [http://www.what-the-hell-is-hell.com], January, 2009.

44. Thomas Thayer, The Origins and History of the Doctrine of Endless Punishment (Kessinger Publishing: Montana, 2007) p. 74-97.

45. Ibid., p. 81-82.

46. Matthias Bejer, A Violent God-image: an introduction to the work of Eugen Drewermann (Continuum: New York, 2004).

47. Cambridge Master of Arts, The Bible history of Satan. Is he a fallen angel? (1858). [http://www.google.com/books?id=EqkCAAAAQAAJ&dq=The+Bible +history+of+Satan.+Is+he+a+fallen+angel%3F+By+a+Cambridge+mas ter+of+arts]

48. Bart D. Ehrman, Whose Words Is it? The story behind who changed the New Testament and Why (Continuum International Publishing Group LTD: New York, 2008), p. 10.

49. Translated by George Eliot, The Life of Jesus: critically examined (C. Blanchard, 1860), p. 41-54.

50. John S. Vaughan, Concerning the Holy Bible: Its use and abuse (Benziger Bros: New York, 1904), p. 11-12.

51. Peter Stravinskas, The Catholic Church and the Bible (Ignatius Press: San Francisco, 1996), p. 17.

52. Bart D. Ehrman, <u>The Orthodox Corruption of Scripture: the effect of early Christological controversies in the text of the New Testament</u> (Oxford University Press: USA, 1996), p. xi.

53. Mark D. Roberts, <u>Can We Trust the Gospels? investigating the reliability of Mathew, Mark, Luke, and John</u> (Good News Publishers: Illinois, 2007), p. 27.

54. John S. Vaughan, <u>Concerning the Holy Bible: Its use and abuse</u> (Benziger Bros: New York, 1904), p. 12.

55. DC Parker and Jeff Childers, <u>Transmission and Reception: New Testament text-critical and exegetical studies</u> (Gorgias Press: New Jersey, 2006), p. 40.

56. Mark D. Roberts, <u>Can We Trust the Gospels?: investigating the reliability of Mathew, Mark, Luke, and John </u>(Good News Publishers: Illinois, 2007), p. 28.

57. John S. Vaughan, <u>Concerning the Holy Bible: Its use and abuse</u> (Benziger Bros: New York, 1904), p. 14.

58. Bart D. Ehrman, <u>Misquoting Jesus; the story behind who changed the Bible and why</u> (Harper San Francisco: San Francisco, 2007), p. 5.

59. Bart D. Ehrman, <u>Whose Words Is it? The story behind who changed the New Testament and Why</u> (Harper San Francisco: San Francisco, 2005), p.7.

60. Ibid.

61. Bart D. Ehrman, <u>Lost Scriptures: books that did not make it into the New Testament</u> (Oxford University Press: Oxford; New York, 2003).

62. Christians Timothy David Barnes, Constantine and Eusebius (Harvard University Press: Massachusetts, 1981), p. 216.

63. David L. Dungan, Constantine's Bible: politics and the making of the New Testament (Fortress Press: Philadelphia, 2006), pg 112.

64. Bart D. Ehrman, Truth and Fiction in the Da Vinci Code: a historian reveals what we really know about Jesus, Mary Magdalene, and Constantine (Oxford University: New York, 2004), p. 98.

65. Alexander Campbell and John Baptist Purcell, A Debate on the Roman Catholic Religion: held in Sycamore Street Meeting House, Cincinnati, from the 13th to the 21st of January, 1837 (J.A. James, 1837), p. 55.

66. Max Arthur Macauliffe, The Sikh Religion, Volume 1 (Forgotten Books, 2008), p. 60.
[http://www.google.com/books?id=E0UwOOjrjGAC&dq=The+Sikh+Religion]

67. David L. Dungan, Constantine's Bible: politics and the making of the New Testament (Fortress Press: Philadelphia, 2006), p. 112.

68. Ibid., p. 109.

69. Ibid., p. 116.

70. William Anderson Scott, The Bible and Politic: or, An humble plea for equal, perfect, absolute religious freedom, and against all sectarianism in our public schools (H.H. Bancroft, 1859), p. 83.

71. David L. Dungan, Constantine's Bible: politics and the making of the New Testament (Fortress Press: Philadelphia, 2006), p. 102.

72. Ibid., p. 96.

73. Ibid., p. 125.

74. Adrian Thatcher, The Savage Text: the use and abuse of the Bible (Wiley-Blackwell: United Kingdom, 2008), p. 3-4.

75. Alexander Campbell and John Baptist Purcell, A Debate on the Roman Catholic Religion: held in Sycamore Street Meeting House, Cincinnati, from the 13th to the 21st of January, 1837 (J.A. James, 1837), p. 263.

76. John S. Vaughan, Concerning the Holy Bible: Its use and abuse (Benziger Bros: New York, 1904), p. 81.

77. Jack Nelson-Pallmeyer, Is Religion Killing Us?: violence in the Bible and the Quran (Continuum International Publishing Group: New York, 2005), p.32.

78. Ibid., p. 34-35.

79. Richard Heber Newton, The Right and Wrong Uses of the Bible (John W. Lovell, 1883), p. 43. [http://www.google.com/books?id=bww-AAAAYAAJ&dq=The+Right+and+Wrong+Uses+of+the+Bible]

80. Joseph Ennemoser, The History of Magic. Trans. By W. Howitt (1854), p. 132. [http://www.google.com/books?id=dhoHAAAAQAAJ&dq=The+history +of+magic,+tr.+by+W.+Howitt.+To+which+is+added+an+appendix+of +the+most+remarkable+and+best+authenticated+stories+of+apparitions +%5B%26c.%5D+selected+by+M.+Howitt]

81. John Barton and Julia Bowden, The Original Story: God, Israel, and the world (Wm. B. Eerdmans Publishing: Michigan, 2005), p. 262. / S.A. Nigosian, The Zoroastrian Faith: tradition and modern research (McGill-Queen's University Press: Montreal, 1993) p. 71-97.

82. Alexander Heidel, The Gilgamesh Epic and Old Testament Parallels (University of Chicago: Chicago, 1949).

83. (editor and translator) Stephanie Dalley, Myths from Mesopotamia: creation, the flood, Gilgamesh, and others (Oxford University Press: New York, 1998).

84. Remi Brague, The Law of God: the philosophical history of an idea. Trans. by Lydia G. Cochrane (University of Chicago Press: United States, 2007), p. 70-71.

85. Ibid., p. 71.

LOVE
BE LOVED
LIVE

Love God and be a God Conscious
Citizen. In God's Mercy, the Lord will
send the Spirit. God's Spirit truthfully
teaches, and the Spirit can give The Name
of God while activating the Word within.
The Word's resonance allows the "I" to
experience the absolute reality. That
experience can bestow salvation (union
with The Great Architect) on any living
thing. A permanent love, in the truest
sense, can be achieved.

God's Word, God's Spirit, and God's Name are unveiled in the book, ***Sikhie Secrets***.

46323471R00067

Made in the USA
Middletown, DE
28 July 2017